Believing and Being

© Aberystwyth University, 2015

These materials are subject to copyright and no part of this publication may be reproduced or published without the written permission of the copyright holder.

Published by CAA, Aberystwyth University, Plas Gogerddan, Aberystwyth, SY23 3EB (www.aber.ac.uk/caa).

Sponsored by the Welsh Government

ISBN: 978-1-84521-570-5

Edited by Delyth Ifan
Designed by Richard Huw Pritchard
Printed by Cambrian Printers

All rights reserved.

Acknowledgements

Unless otherwise indicated, all Scripture quotations are taken from the Holy Bible, New Living Translation, copyright © 1996, 2004, 2007 by Tyndale House Foundation. Used by permission of Tyndale House Publishers, Inc., Carol Stream, Illinois 60188. All rights reserved.
p. 16, Activity 14, RE Today Services; p. 17, Basil Zangare; pp. 36 and 78, Scripture quotations, Holy Bible, New International Version; p. 56, image, Lion Publishing, 1985; pp. 58-59, images from Hea Woo's story, Open Doors UK; pp. 87-88, images and story of Anne Frank, Liepman Agency on behalf of Anne Frank Fonds; text from THE DIARY OF A YOUNG GIRL: THE DEFINITIVE EDITION (pp. 258, 317, 409, 419) by Anne Frank, edited by Otto H Frank and Mirjam Pressler, translated by Susan Massotty (Viking, 1997) copyright © The Anne Frank-Fonds, Basle, Switzerland, 1991. English translation copyright © Doubleday a division of Bantam Doubleday Dell Publishing Group Inc, 1995.

Every effort has been made to trace and acknowledge ownership of copyright. The publisher will be pleased to make suitable arrangements with any copyright holders who have not been contacted.

Thanks to Christine Hannaby, Jason Rees and Brian Ward for their valuable guidance.

CONTENTS

SKILLS SHEET	04
INTRODUCTION	05
UNIT 1: THE POWER OF BELIEF	06
UNIT 2: DOES MY CULTURE DEFINE ME?	24
UNIT 3: DOES FAITH STAND THE TEST?	50
UNIT 4: FAITH IN A MULTICULTURAL SOCIETY	68

SKILLS SHEET

Level	Engage		Explore		Express	
		Fundamental questions: These are the questions that the unit aims to answer. The unit may contain smaller questions (FQ's) to help you think, and the answers one person gives may not be the same as someone else. You should be able to give a reason why a person holds that belief.	Describe and begin to explain beliefs, teachings and practices (BTP). Give specific examples of beliefs and teachings in practice. Begin to identify similarities and differences *within* religions.	**Practices** A focus on the actions that a person will take based on his/her beliefs	Explain in simple terms your feelings, actions and opinions and how they differ from others.	**Questions:** Whilst studying the unit you will be able to explain your opinion on the topics covered. You may explain why you act the way you do, and you should be able to understand, describe or explain why other people act in the ways they do.
	Discuss your own response and other's responses to fundamental questions (FQ's).					
	Express and justify ideas and opinions about fundamental questions (FQ's) (in the light of investigations and experiences).		Make links between beliefs, teachings and practices (BTP) describing the impact. Identify similarities and differences *within* **and** *across* religions.	**Teachings** A focus on the teachings that affect a person's beliefs	Explain how your feelings, actions and opinions affect your own life. Describe how the feelings, actions and opinions of others affect their own lives.	
	Draw on various sources and your own experiences to present a response to the fundamental questions (FQ's).		Use your understanding of the links between beliefs, teachings and practices (BTP) to understand religion. Explain differing religious viewpoints and beliefs, teachings and practices (BTP).		Explain the relationship between your own beliefs and actions and explain the relationship between the beliefs and actions of others.	
	Investigate fundamental questions (FQ's) from a variety of perspectives and begin to draw reasoned conclusions.		Apply a wide range of religious concepts to a variety of beliefs, teachings and practices (BTP). Explain and justify reasons for the range of viewpoints held by religious people.	**Beliefs** A focus on the belief that a person may have	Consider the implications of your beliefs and actions, comparing them to other people and drawing conclusions.	

➡ ➡ **Increased level of challenge and achievement** ➡ ➡

INTRODUCTION

Themes and Fundamental Questions

This book explores the fascinating world of beliefs and believing. Although the focus will be on religious beliefs, it is important to remember that the lives of each and everyone of us involve some kind of beliefs or believing. Much of everyday life has things that we expect to be the way they are, or to happen in a particular pattern. It is how we manage to get on with our lives easily and happily.

That is why the book is entitled '**Believing and Being**' – because the things that we believe (about ourselves, about other people, about the world) give us a framework which helps us to make sense of our lives, and the things that happen in them.

The book has four themes:

1. The power of belief

This section tries to think about the way the things we believe affect the way we live our lives and relate to other people, and the things that happen in our lives.

2. Does my culture define me?

Here we consider the effects of our location, culture and heritage on our beliefs, and whether this matters.

3. Does faith stand the test?

When it comes to religious faith or belief, people often think it really matters to them. So we consider how living with other people in our society today tests our personal beliefs, and also how the things that happen to us may also put a strain on our beliefs.

4. Faith in a multicultural society

This section looks at the issues about keeping a personal faith in a multicultural setting, without losing any sense of the integrity (or good character) of a faith, but accepting that the different faith and beliefs of others also matter to them.

Four fundamental questions are considered as we go through the chapters:

FUNDAMENTAL QUESTIONS

i. Why are there different faiths?
ii. Is religious heritage helpful?
iii. Does faith matter?
iv. How do different world views affect your belief?

UNIT 1

THE POWER OF BELIEF

Engage with fundamental questions:

What is belief?
How powerful are beliefs?
What is an ultimate question?

Explore Beliefs,

- Why people believe what they do.
- Why beliefs can be a powerful force in people's lives.
- How specific beliefs can influence the way a person reacts and behaves.
- Belief and faith have a sound foundation.

Teachings

- Sikh and Muslim (and possibly Christian or Hindu) teachings about:
  a) finding peace and harmony;
  b) whether God watches us or not;
  c) what God is like;
  d) prayer;
  e) what happens after death.

and Practices

- What people do to strengthen/develop their beliefs/faith.
- How believers act in situations because of their beliefs and their religion's teachings.

Express:

Using your own opinions, along with what you have found out …

How do beliefs affect your own life?
What is the effect of belief in responding to situations and to others?
Does everyone have beliefs that shape their lives?
Can beliefs change as people change?

The things people believe – about themselves, or about other people – can be really powerful, affecting everything they think, do and say. Sometimes this can be a good thing, and sometimes it can lead to unpleasant and harmful experiences.

You may be asked to complete a number of activities to help explore just how powerful beliefs can be. For the activity undertaken, consider how they help us to understand the links between our beliefs and our actions

ACTIVITY 4

Look at the statements of belief below. Decide which might lead to good outcomes or benefits, and which might be unpleasant or harmful. If there are any statements that you are not sure which way they might lead, explain your dilemma.

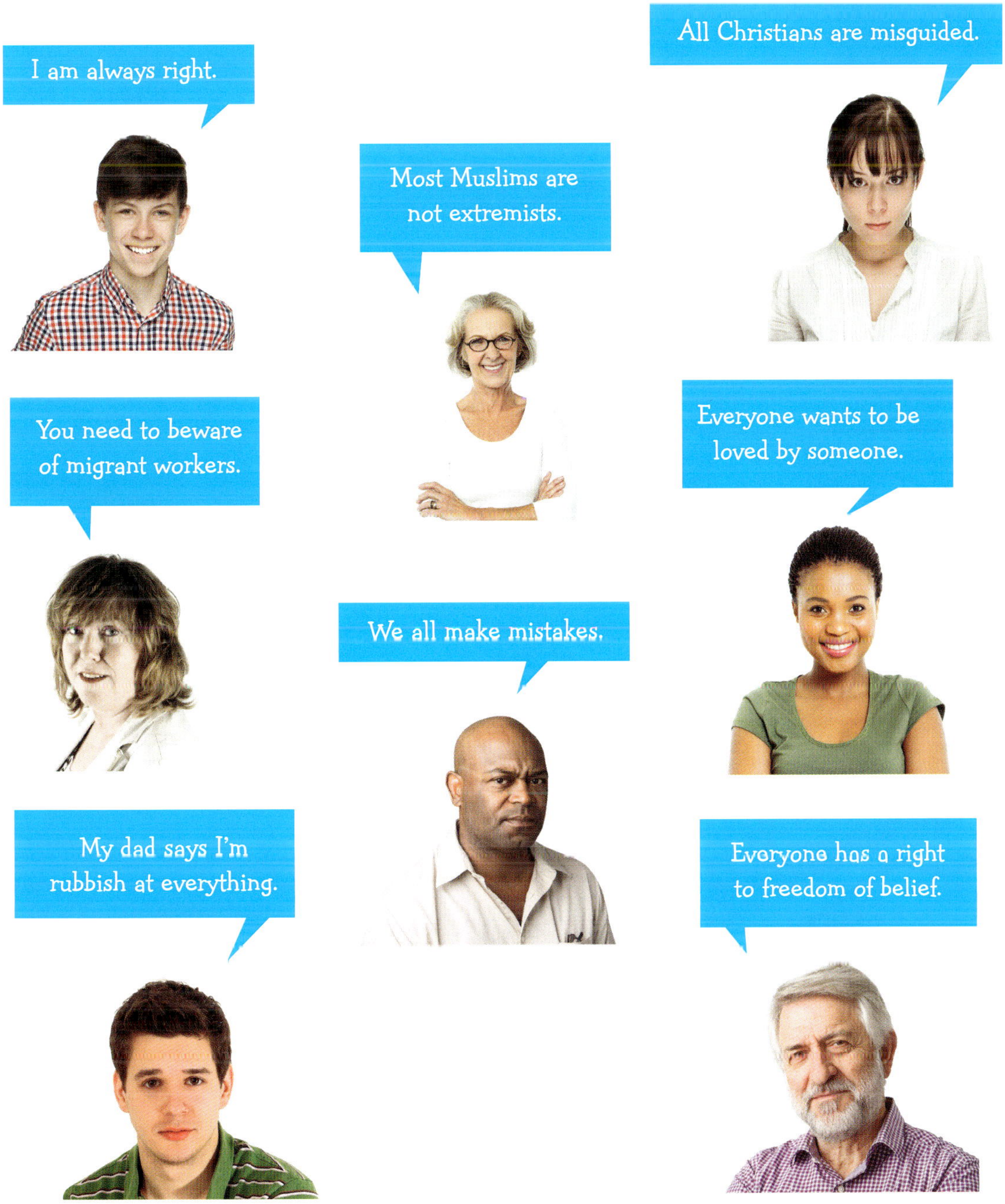

- I am always right.
- All Christians are misguided.
- Most Muslims are not extremists.
- You need to beware of migrant workers.
- Everyone wants to be loved by someone.
- We all make mistakes.
- My dad says I'm rubbish at everything.
- Everyone has a right to freedom of belief.

ACTIVITY 5

Complete this sentence, on the basis of the activities and discussions you have had so far:
'Beliefs have power because ...

What is belief?

There is a difference between statements of belief, statements of fact, and statements that are just opinions.

BELIEF: something you think is true, but there is no proof that you can provide, e.g. "I believe that God exists."

FACT: something that can be proved to be true or correct, e.g. "There are eleven words and fifty two letters in this statement."

OPINION: something that you like or prefer, and is a matter of personal taste, e.g. "There is too much football on television and not enough rugby."

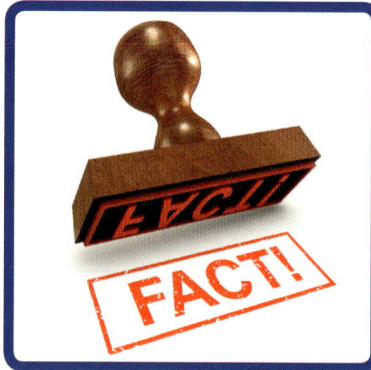

ACTIVITY 6

Write your own examples of statements which are beliefs, statements which are facts and statements which are opinions. Share your ideas with a partner.

- Jesus is the Son of God and Saviour of the World.
- Telling the truth is a basic value that all should follow.
- All humans are equal, and none should be treated unjustly or unfairly.
- God has no form or features, but is the Truth.
- It is wrong to kill animals for food.
- Not all beliefs are religious beliefs. Sometimes people believe in things which they think are especially important, or which they see as values regardless of religion. People often use the word 'belief' when they are really just saying what they think – so it is more like their opinion.
- Everyone has the right to freedom of belief.
- Brahma is the creator, Shiva the destroyer, Vishnu the preserver.
- There is no God but Allah, and Muhammad is his prophet.
- No one should take another person's life.

Before proceeding further, complete the 'Beliefs' chart **ACTIVITY 7**, and keep it until you have completed the first section of this book.

Specific religious beliefs can be identified by including some reference to the following sorts of things:

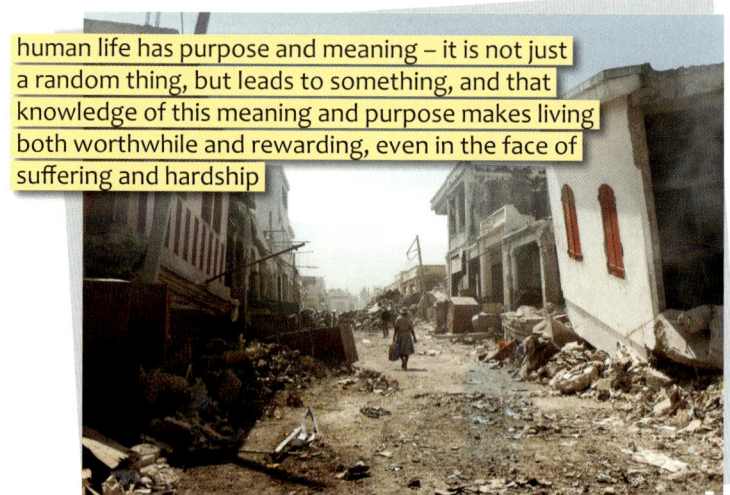

a spiritual dimension to life – that there is more than just the physical

a divine being, or creator, or 'ultimate truth' behind the universe

human life has purpose and meaning – it is not just a random thing, but leads to something, and that knowledge of this meaning and purpose makes living both worthwhile and rewarding, even in the face of suffering and hardship

life being sacred, and of special value above other things

there is a life after death - beyond the physical and the current body we inhabit

Naturally, religions have beliefs about many aspects of life and living which derive from the beliefs about ultimate questions such as those mentioned above, although these may not be obvious as religious beliefs at first. Many religions have teachings about giving to charity, and many non-religious people also have beliefs about this topic.

ACTIVITY 8

Look at the statements below and carry out the activity your teacher directs you to do. You will be asked to say whether you agree or disagree with some of the statements, to think about who might have said a particular statement, what experiences might have led them to say it, and what a specific religious person might say about it.

Giving to Charity

A	It is the government's job to look after people who need help. There should be no need to have any charities.
B	The Lottery fund is supposed to be helping charities, so why should they give it to things like opera and the theatre? It should go to people who really need it.
C	Charity begins at home. I spend every penny I get.
D	Charity begins at home. I need every penny I get.
E	Giving to charity is an important part of the way I show my love for God.
F	I don't give to charity. It's just another form of begging.
G	If some of these people stopped being lazy, and got up and did some things for themselves, they wouldn't need charity.
H	I believe in helping others in need by giving to charity because, after all, we all were created by God and he cares about us all.
I	I'm sick of having a collection tin pushed in my face every time I go shopping – there's always some charity or other after your money.
J	I feel good about giving money to charity.
K	I think the better-off should always help those who need it as a way of showing that they are blessed by God.
L	Charity is not only money – you can help people in other ways.
M	You never know when you might need someone to be charitable to you, so I give a bit to charity – just in case.
N	Nobody does anything for nothing. Those charity workers must be getting something out of it.
O	Big businesses and famous people should give a lot more than they do. They only give to charity to get their names in the papers.
P	God wants justice in the world so it is important that I try to help others and make the world a fairer place.

Taken from *Literate RE* by Pamela Draycott. Copyright © 2006 RE Today Services. Used by permission.

What's the difference between 'belief' and 'faith'?

Here are some statements where the words 'believe' and 'faith' are used. Work out the difference in meaning, and then begin to identify the difference between 'belief' and 'faith'.

I believe that there is a silver lining to every cloud.

I have a faith that gives me security.

I believe that there is a God.

I have faith in God.

I believe in technology.

I put my faith in technology.

I believe that you are more than capable.

I have faith in your abilities.

I have absolute faith in my friends.

I believe that friends help each other.

You might have discovered that one of the differences is that faith requires belief and trust. When it is not possible to prove something, or to know exactly if it is true or not, then faith is the trusting that it is there, that it is true.

ACTIVITY 9

Try out one or more of the trust games that are in the teachers' guide.

So if you believe, or have faith, does that mean you are spiritual?

You may not be sure whether or not you are a spiritual person, so check out your 'spiritual identity' by completing Activity 10.

ACTIVITY 10

Use your own copy of the chart below to measure your spirituality.

Spiritual? Me? A quiz to explore spirituality

Work by yourself. Choose ONE reply to each question. Use the copy of the chart you've been given to record your answers. Another chart will help you work out your scores.

A = agree strongly   B = agree a bit   C = disagree a bit   D = disagree completely

	Sixteen spiritual signals: which ones matter to you?	A	B	C	D
1	Music matters to me because through my music I can get my feelings tuned up and my life in harmony.				
2	Other people matter to me because friends and family are the main meaning and purpose in my life.				
3	I'm not bothered about the natural world – animals, birds, streams and mountains. My way of life doesn't need the green.				
4	I believe in something more than just atoms and matter. I might not call this 'God', but there's more to life than science.				
5	Silence and time alone are important to help me feel OK about life. I like thinking deeply about myself.				
6	I don't believe that a partner and a love life makes you happy. You can be happy alone. 'Love' can make you unhappy too.				
7	It is interesting to find out about the world of nature, evolution, where we come from and how the body works. This is exciting.				
8	God doesn't exist. There's no such person. It's all in people's imagination. It's good to be certain about atheism. It's right.				
9	Sometimes I am amazed at life: the ideas, passions and things I can do make me wonder, 'Why do I deserve this?'				
10	If you have a successful family, then that's a successful life. One of my top wishes is to make a good family when I grow up.				
11	I get peace and calm from the outdoor life. I love the world of nature. Rivers, wind, lightning and the sea make me feel alive.				
12	I just don't care about God at all. I'm not really an atheist, but it simply doesn't bother me. I don't ever think about God.				
13	Being born is a gift. And a priceless gift too. I'm grateful for it.				
14	I am a good friend, and I have good friends.				
15	When we die, our bodies rot away, and go back to the dust we came from. This doesn't scare me. Flowers grow on graves.				
16	I have felt, at least once in my life, that I was in touch with a power or a presence different from my 'everyday self'.				

When you have completed the chart, use the score chart you've been given to work out your 'spiritual identity'. Discuss with a partner whether the interpretations fit, and complete the evaluation of the spiritual identity quiz. Then do the final part of the activity – the 'My ideas, my images, my questions' diagram.

What do you believe?

So far we have thought about beliefs and how they influence our thinking and acting, and we have tried to learn what is meant by 'belief' and 'faith'. We have also thought about spiritual identity. Now we turn to thinking about what you yourself believe.

I wonder!
I wonder why people are here on the Earth,
I wonder why there is death and birth.
I wonder what is the point of living?
Why are we taking? And why are we giving?

These key questions have puzzled humans.
Why the world's here, why it began?
Why are there wars and why do we fight?
Why are things wrong? And why are things right?

These key questions have puzzled us so.
What are the answers, does anyone know?
Why is there living and why is there dying?
Why are some people laughing and some people crying?

Why are some countries rich and some countries poor?
What is this thing 'LIFE' and what's it all for?
Is there a heaven up in the sky?
And where do we all go when we die?

(Composed by a pupil during a RE lesson!)

ACTIVITY 11

Write a paragraph stating your own beliefs. Have a look through the fundamental questions below, and try to include something about these issues in your statement of belief. Add other things that are important to you.

- Why are we here?
- Where are we going?
- What is the meaning of life?
- How did the universe begin?
- What happens when we die?
- How do we work out the best way to behave in life?
- Is there a God or ultimate power?
- Are we responsible for ensuring that the world's resources are preserved?
- Why is there suffering in the world?
- Why is there injustice and unfairness in life?

ACTIVITY 12

Once you have completed Activity 11, discuss with a partner your statements of belief. What things did you have in common, and what things did you differ on? Discuss why you have these similarities and differences.

ACTIVITY 13

Following your discussion with a partner, choose one of the areas on which you differed, and write an article explaining and defending your belief. Try to think of all the questions and counter arguments to your belief, and make sure you answer them all in your article.

Ultimate questions – no easy answers

It is difficult to provide answers to most of the really big questions in life. Sometimes it is because it is very difficult to 'prove' beyond any doubt that the things we say in answer to the question/s are true or definite. For example, it is difficult to provide answers to questions about the beginning of the universe, because it is very difficult to find information and evidence from the beginning of time!

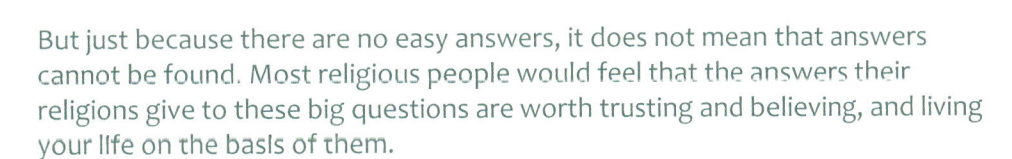

But just because there are no easy answers, it does not mean that answers cannot be found. Most religious people would feel that the answers their religions give to these big questions are worth trusting and believing, and living your life on the basis of them.

The reason for their confidence is that through the experiences and testimony of others – sometimes people who have lived many generations before them – there is a lot of evidence about the value of the beliefs. When their own personal experience of faith and trust is added to this, just like you had in the trust games you played earlier, it all begins to give a strength to the answers that their religion provides.

This does not mean that it is easy, just that there is a basis for trusting the beliefs, and living out your life from them. As you gain experience and confidence, so your trust develops and your faith is strengthened, even at times when it feels as if things count against your beliefs.

Look at these two illustrations of trust, even when things appear to be different.

The resistance fighter and the stranger

It was war time and a small country was occupied, overrun by its neighbour's dictator and army. A resistance group tried to keep hope alive.

One night, a young woman in the resistance met a stranger who impressed her deeply. They talked all night, sharing their hopes and dreams of future freedom. The stranger told her that he too was a member of the resistance, in fact, he was the leader of it. He urged her to have faith in him no matter what happened. The resistance fighter was totally convinced of the stranger's sincerity and promised to trust and follow him.

Although they never met again in a situation where they could have a private conversation, she often saw the stranger helping members of the resistance. She would say to her friends, 'I know him, he's a good man, he's on our side.'

But sometimes the stranger seemed to be helping the enemy. She would see him in police uniform, chatting to the dictator and even handing over patriots to the occupying army. Her friends became angry and accused the stranger of treachery. But the resistance fighter would not join in: 'He knows best,' she would say, 'he's doing all he can. Trust him.'

Sometimes she asked the stranger for help and received it. She was grateful. But at other times when she asked, there was no help, and sometimes no answer. Still she would say: 'The stranger knows best. I don't doubt him. I know him. He is on our side.'

'What will it take before you admit that you are wrong about him?' her friends often asked angrily. But she refused to answer; she would not put the stranger to the test. She trusted him. They argued, 'If that's what you mean by being on our side, the sooner the stranger goes over to the enemy, the better.' But still she would not give up her trust in the stranger.

From J Mackley and C Johnson (eds.) RE in Practice: Is it True? (CEM 2000). The story of the resistance fighter is adapted from an original idea by Basil Mitchell in New Essays in Philosophical Thinking, ed. A Flew and A Mackintyre, London 1955.

ACTIVITY 14

a) What makes the resistance fighter trust the stranger?
b) How does the resistance fighter know that the stranger is telling her the truth?
c) What events might have made her doubt the stranger?
d) Why does she not doubt or test the stranger despite these events?
e) Why do you think religious believers refuse to test or doubt God?
f) Suggest some everyday examples of times when we need to take people at face value and trust what they say.
g) What would life be like if we never trusted anyone or anything?

Footprints in the sand

One night I had a dream – I dreamed I was walking along the beach with the Lord and across the sky flashed scenes from my life.
For each scene I noticed two sets of footprints, one belonged to me and the other to the Lord.

When the last scene of my life flashed before me, I looked back at the footprints in the sand.
I noticed that many times along the path of my life, there was only one set of footprints.

I also noticed that it happened at the very lowest and saddest times in my life.
This really bothered me and I questioned the Lord about it.
"Lord, you said that once I decided to follow you, you would walk with me all the way, but I have noticed that during the most troublesome times in my life there is only one set of footprints."

"I don't understand why in times when I needed you most, you should leave me."
The Lord replied, "My precious, precious child, I love you and I would never, never leave you during your times of trial and suffering.

"When you saw only one set of footprints it was then that I carried you."

© Mary Stevenson

ACTIVITY 15

a) How do you think this poem makes believers feel?
b) What difference does it make to the way they face difficult times in the future?
c) Who or what do you trust in, especially when things are difficult and testing?

Although there may not be easy answers to the big questions that we all face in our lives, religious believers are confident that their faith is not a blind leap in the dark, but a step taken as a result of faith that is based on good evidence and sound experience. Despite not knowing all, or any answers, when there is something you can trust in and be sure of, you will have confidence to face life and its challenges.

ACTIVITY 16

Ultimate questions – Muslim and Sikh responses

In pairs or small groups, look at the 10 cards of statements from young Muslims and Sikhs. Firstly, match the cards into pairs – a Muslim comment and a Sikh comment about the same thing or issue. Secondly, decide what ultimate question the young believers were answering by their statement, and record them in the grid you have been given. Thirdly, add your own answers in the column provided on the grid. Fourthly, **for an extended homework:** (a) research into answers to the same five big questions from Christianity or Hinduism and (b) choose **one** of the big questions, and write an extended essay answer to it, making sure you include at least **two** different religious responses, the range of questions that are raised by the issue, and your own personal thinking about it.

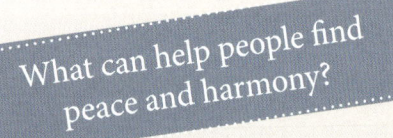

- What can help people find peace and harmony?
- What do you think about prayer to God?
- What happens when a person dies?
- Is God watching us?
- What is God like?

'You find peace in a mosque. God always looks after us.'

'I think God is good, and He is sending special people down to tell us how to live.'

'I believe God is always watching on what we do, and how we treat each other.'

'Be fair and do not judge people. Sometimes forgive and get on with life.'

Does it affect my actions?

We have looked into beliefs and why people believe what they do. But we need to think about whether what a person believes makes a difference. At the beginning of this unit we saw that believing something has a certain power or force which can persuade us to do something we would not otherwise do, or appreciate something that we might have missed at first sight.

Take the case of a man who, when sailing with his family on their boat, had to risk his own life to save that of his family. When the boat capsized in a sudden squall, he told his family to hang on to the upturned boat while he went to raise the alarm. He swam to the shore, which ended up being a mile and a half away. He climbed a treacherous cliff face, because the current in the water had landed him on that part of the shore, and he had no time or strength to battle with the current to get to an easier shoreline. On reaching the top of the cliff, he ran nearly half a mile to a farmhouse where he saw some lights. There he was able to get help, and his family were eventually rescued.

Now, if you had asked the man to swim a mile and a half in rough seas, climb a treacherous cliff, and run half a mile – just for the sake of doing it – he probably could not have done it. But because the lives of his family were at stake, he found depths of strength that he did not realise he had. He believed he needed to do everything he could to save his family, and that enabled him to keep going beyond normal limits.

This is an extreme example of how belief affects actions. But, if you think about it, whatever you believe about something, it will affect the way you react or the things you do in that connection.

ACTIVITY 17

Look at the 'Codes of lifestyle' charts on pages 20-21 for the three religions, and then consider how each of the characters in the scenarios that follow would react **in the light of** their religion's teachings and beliefs. Explain clearly the reason for your choice of action, and the issues or conflicts that might arise for the believer.

Christianity - codes of lifestyle

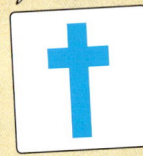

- Jesus said that the way to be happy and blessed is to:
  - be open to God, and to other people around us
  - be gentle and kind in our dealings with people
  - always be fair and honest
  - ensure others are treated well and fairly
  - show forgiveness whenever we can
  - live good lives at all times
  - be peacemakers, helping others to be friends and work together (based on the Beatitudes [Matthew 5: 3-12; Luke 6: 20-23])

- The Bible also teaches the importance of sharing (e.g. John the Baptist taught that those with two coats should share one with those who have none).

- Giving to charity has always been important and some Christians give a regular amount each month to a charity (often a tenth of their income, called 'a tithe').

- The Bible states: 'The love of money is the root of all evil." (1 Timothy 6: 10)

- Retaliation to others who harm or mistreat you is not helpful. Jesus said, 'Pray for those who are against you'.

- Jesus' own example was one of love, compassion and forgiveness to others; He taught to love one's neighbour as oneself, and He called His followers to be peacemakers.

- Jesus also said that His followers should be willing to forgive others over and over again.

- The Parable of the Good Samaritan shows that it is important to treat others how you would wish to be treated yourself. ('The Golden Rule: Matthew 7:12 – Do for others what you want them to do for you.)

Sikhism

Hinduism - codes of lifestyle

- Hinduism teaches that it is important _not_ to:
  - harm or destroy anything: ahimsa (harmlessness)
  - tell untruths
  - take things that do not belong to you (steal)
  - allow sexual desires to become too strong (lust)
  - eat or drink too much (greed)
  - be jealous of or envy what others have or do

- Hinduism teaches that it _is important to_:
  - forgive others willingly
  - be content with your life and living
  - be clean or pure, inside and out
  - be non-violent in your actions and behaviour
  - always be truthful

Buddhism - codes of lifestyle

- The 10 precepts (or guidelines for living) give clear directions –

  For all Buddhists
  to:
  ~ avoid harming or taking life: show love and kindness to all living beings and things
  ~ avoid taking what is not given: be generous to others, and willing to share what you have
  ~ avoid harmful sexual activity: sex should be controlled and not in excess, and never cause suffering to others
  ~ avoid telling untruths: be honest and open with everyone and in all situations
  ~ avoid taking alcohol and drugs, which cloud the mind: it is good to be as alert as possible, and be aware of what is going on around you.

  For monks only
  to:
  ~ avoid eating after midday
  ~ avoid dancing, singing and watching unsuitable entertainments
  ~ avoid using perfumes and personal decorations or jewellery
  ~ avoid sleeping in luxury beds
  ~ avoid handling gold and silver

- Compassion, kindness and love for all human beings are at the heart of Buddhism.
- Helping others is one of the most important Buddhist virtues.
- Inner peace is the greatest victory and achievement.
- Buddha's own example was to give up a life of riches; he taught that craving for material wealth leads to suffering.
- The middle way is the aim of life – not to have too much or too little.
- It is important to gain money honestly.
- The main duty in Buddhism is sila – keeping the precepts of behaviour; each person is responsible for their own actions and their consequences.

~ be tolerant of others
~ value learning, and make all efforts to increase your knowledge and understanding

- Wealth is loaned by God, and so it is important how it is used.
- Personal wealth should be gained honestly and lawfully.
- Material possession are not of lasting value.
- The inner spiritual life and doing one's duty (dharma) are the main focus of life; it is through the performance of these that <u>moksha</u> is achieved.
- Maintaining a peaceful society and protecting the innocent is important.

Scenario 1

Name: Matthew (known by his friends as 'Matt')

Profile: Matt is a keen sportsman, and likes basketball and athletics (high jump in particular). He attends the local parish church of St John's, and goes to their Youth Group and Young People's Bible Study Group.

He is sometimes 'bullied' and often mocked about his faith by some of his basketball and athletics club friends.

Problem: Recently there has been some serious damage to sports equipment in the club's gym storeroom. Matt has been blamed by some of the others, as a sort of joke because of his faith. Matt did not cause the damage, but to stand up for himself means he will have to 'tell on' some of the others in the team.

How should Matt, as a Christian, deal with this situation?

[Remember to explain clearly the reason for your choice of action and the issues or conflicts that might arise for the believer.]

Scenario 2

Name: Sangmu

Profile: Sangmu is a Buddhist, and is very gifted in art and music. She plays the flute, and has achieved Grade 7. She is liked by most of her classmates, and although top in exams for Art and Music, she is not high up in other exams and grades.

Problem: Whilst completing some artwork after school one day, Sangmu sees a copy of the end of unit Geography exam. It was just on the desk in the room she was in — she didn't go looking for it or expecting to find it. But she did see it, and now knows all the topics for the exam. It would be a great opportunity to do well in that exam.

How should Sangmu, as a Buddhist, deal with this situation?

[Remember to explain clearly the reason for your choice of action, and the issues or conflicts that might arise for the believer.]

Scenario 3

Name: Hemen

Profile: Hemen is a Hindu, the second son of a wealthy business man. He is good at drama, and loves Indian music and dance. He is very skilled on the computer and on play station games, and loves nothing better than challenging his friends to a game. He spends a lot of time helping out at a local branch of the Hindu charity *Food for Life*, and gets a real sense of fulfilment from helping those who come to the centre for help.

Problem: Hemen's dad has given him a special gift of £400, and he can do whatever he likes with it. This was for his achievements in an Indian dance competition, and to acknowledge the work he does with the charity. Hemen planned to use the money to buy the latest PS4, so that he and his friends could enjoy competing with each other. However, the *Food for Life* centre desperately needs funds to help the increasing number of homeless and hungry people coming to them for help.

How should Hemen, as a Hindu, deal with this situation?

[Remember to explain clearly the reason for your choice of action, and the issues or conflicts that might arise for the believer.]

Summing up: The power of belief

We started out by thinking about what beliefs were, and how they differ from facts and opinions. We moved on to consider what we ourselves believe, and then specific religious beliefs and why people believe them. We also thought about the difference between 'belief' and 'faith', and what that difference means. Thinking about the impact of belief on the way people interpret what happens to them in their lives, and the way they respond to events and other people, helped us to understand that what we do believe can have quite an influence on the way we do things, and the way we think. And we can conclude that, for religious people, belief or faith is not some kind of 'blind faith', but something that has a sound foundation, but requires trust and commitment.

UNIT 2
DOES MY CULTURE DEFINE ME?

Engage with fundamental questions:

What makes up a culture?

Does a culture affect a person's beliefs?

Do religious beliefs affect a person's actions?

Explore Beliefs,

- Important people can begin a religion.
- Holy books can influence people's beliefs.
- Circumstances can influence beliefs and actions.

Teachings

- The beginnings and the holy books of the 6 main world religions.
- Difference between Eastern religious views and Western religious views on life after death.

and Practices

- The effect religious belief has, e.g. reading holy books, visiting holy buildings and special places.

Express:

Using your own opinions along with what you have found out ...

What makes up a culture?

How does a culture affect a person's beliefs?

Why do religious beliefs affect a person's actions?

Why do you believe ...?

```
BC/AD
BCE/CE      Celts
                                                          Today
     Birth of Christ
```

Why do you believe what you believe? It's an interesting question. In the previous unit we considered some of our beliefs and why we may believe them. Many beliefs are shared by a group of people. The history and geography of these people may have an important part to play in the beliefs that they have. For example, the Celts had particular beliefs about the world, gods and the afterlife. Historically, they lived between the 8th century and first century BCE. Geographically, they lived in central and northern Europe. We may say that many of these beliefs may be directly linked to their **'culture'**. Does your culture define you?

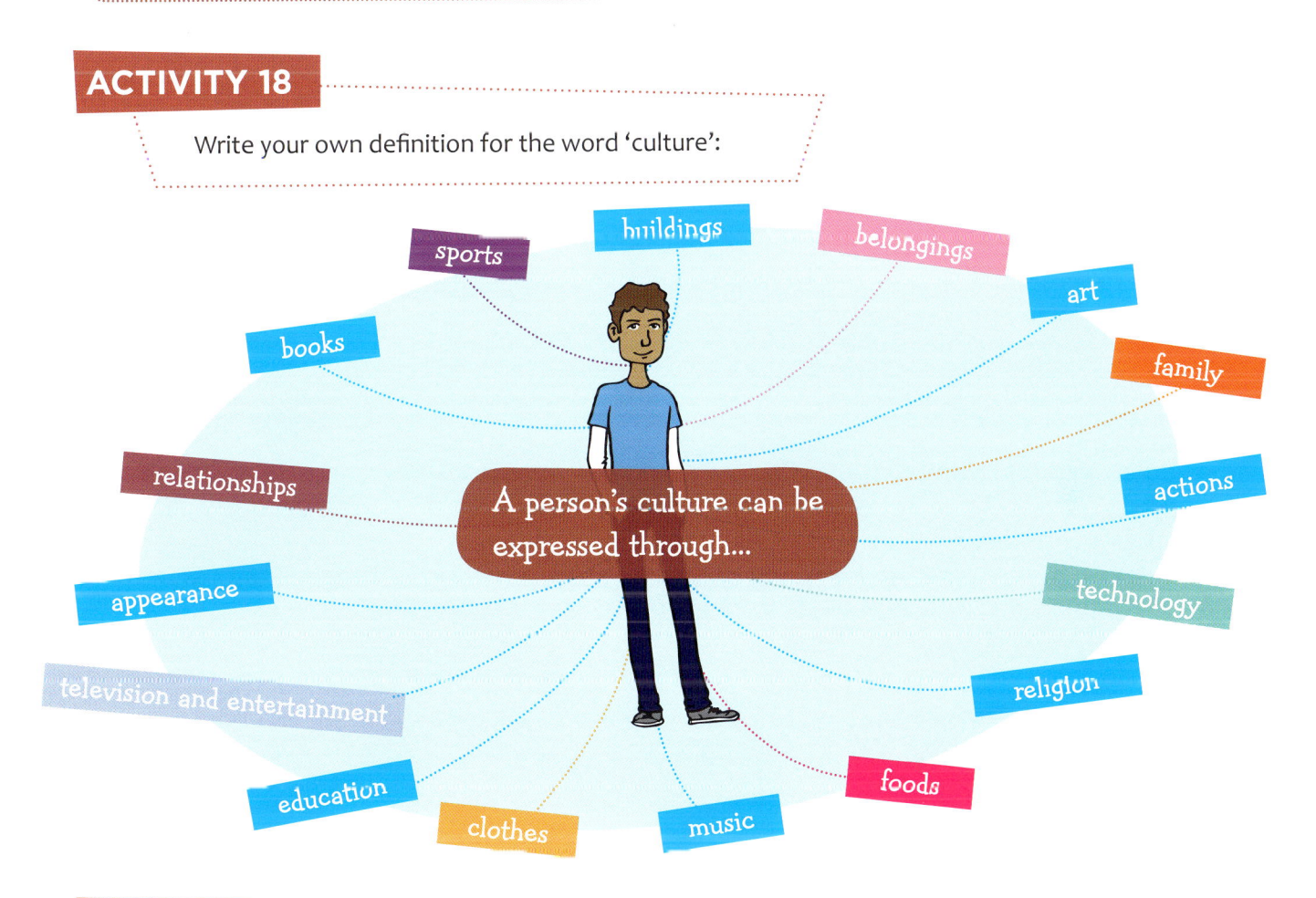

ACTIVITY 18

Write your own definition for the word 'culture':

A person's culture can be expressed through...

- sports
- buildings
- belongings
- art
- books
- family
- relationships
- actions
- appearance
- technology
- television and entertainment
- religion
- education
- foods
- clothes
- music

ACTIVITY 19

a) Choose some of the above headings and write down at least one example for each.
b) Create a digital presentation (e.g. music video) to express your own culture, the culture of Wales or a mixture of both in the early 21st century.
c) Create a summary of your digital presentation describing the images you have used. Explain why they relate either to your culture or Welsh culture in the 21st century.
d) Find other people in your class who have:
   i. very similar examples
   ii. very different examples

Who and what affects my beliefs?

There are many possible influences on a person's beliefs. The views of family and friends will affect us. Events in our lives may change the way we look at the world around us. You could think of each influence as a jigsaw piece making up the whole.

ACTIVITY 20

Think of people or circumstances that have influenced you. Using a picture of the jigsaw head, show the people and the influences that have affected your beliefs. Think about where you place them. Do you listen to some more than others? You could place this one by the ear.

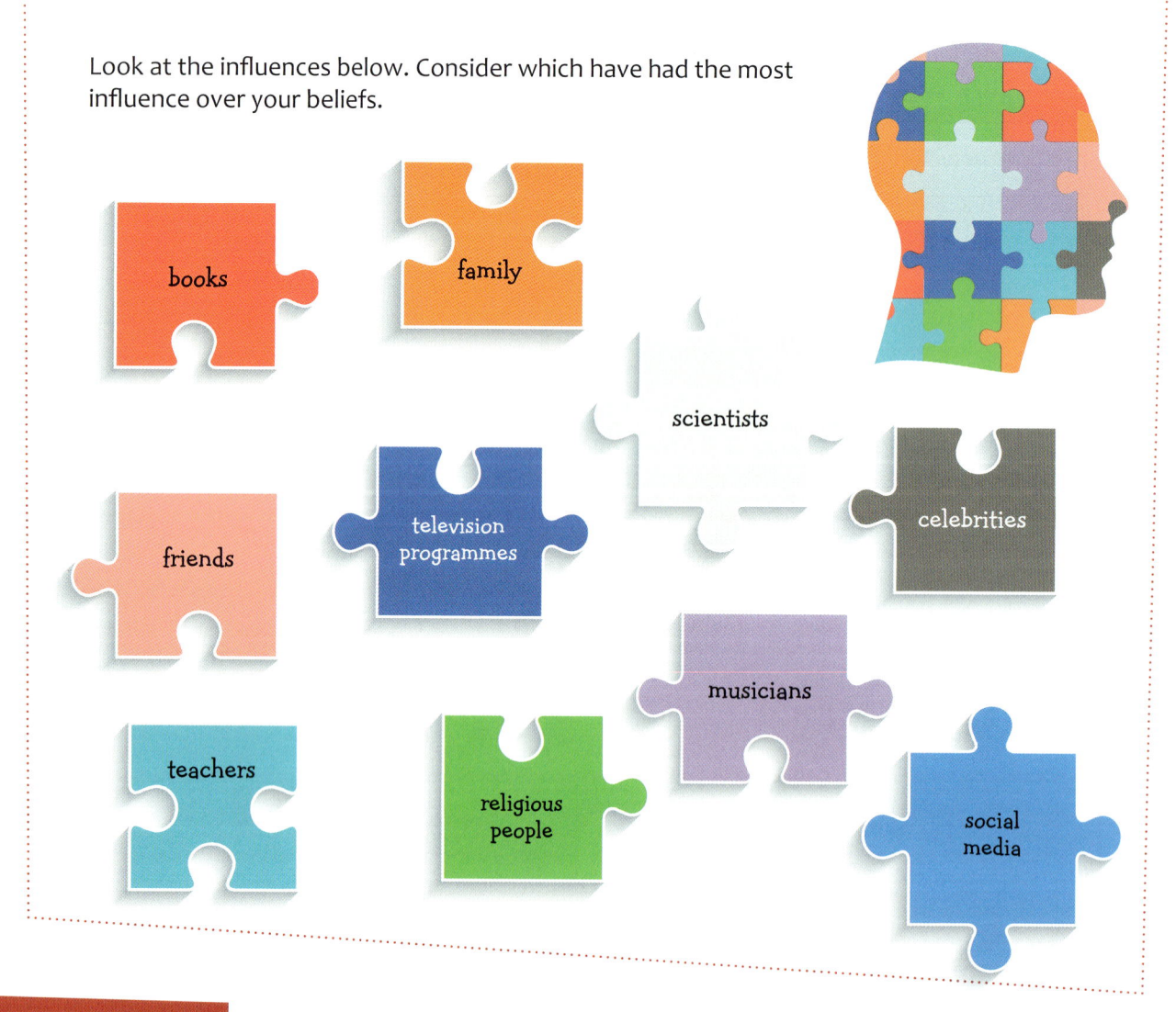

Look at the influences below. Consider which have had the most influence over your beliefs.

- books
- family
- scientists
- friends
- television programmes
- celebrities
- musicians
- teachers
- religious people
- social media

ACTIVITY 21

Diamond nine

a) Rank the influences above in order of importance.

b) Explain your choice of the most important influence and give an example of how it has affected your life.

The story of the Buddha and Muhammad and the influences that affected their lives

Buddha

Siddhartha Gautama, who later became known as the Buddha and the founder of Buddhism, was born a prince, next in-line to be king. His father, King Suddhodana, ensured that the young Siddhartha grew up in luxury, not coming into contact with suffering of any kind. Siddhartha married and had a son, but he wanted to see what life was like outside the palace.

Siddhartha persuaded his servant Channa to drive him to the local town. On his first visit he saw an old man. On the second visit he saw a sick person. On the third visit he saw a dead body in a funeral procession. He had never seen old age, sickness or death before. He was so concerned with suffering that on his fourth visit, seeing a holy man, Siddhartha decided that he would devote his life to finding an end to suffering.

Much of the teaching of Buddhism is devoted to understanding the nature of suffering and trying to end it.

Muhammad

Muhammad, the founder of Islam, never knew his father. His father died before he was born. His mother died when he was six. He lived and grew up in Makkah, working for his uncle. At the age of 25 he met and married a wealthy widow, Khadija.

By the time he was 40 years old, Muhammad would wander into the surrounding hills. Whilst meditating in a cave on Mount Hira, Muhammad was visited by the angel Jibreel/Gabriel who told him to 'recite'. Muhammad began to recite words which he believed were the words of God. The Qur'an is the collection of these words that were given to Muhammad.

Muhammad believed that Allah was the only God to be worshipped, but the people of Makkah worshipped many idols. Muhammad preached the message that he had received to the people of Makkah. Some people believed him, others ignored his teachings.

He moved with his followers to Madinah, gaining more support. Ten years later he returned to Makkah and removed all the idols from the city, ensuring that only people who worshipped Allah lived there. From then on, only Muslims were allowed in the city.

The belief in one god is explained in the Muslim statement of faith, the Shah'adah.

ACTIVITY 22

a) Read the story of either Siddhartha or Muhammad.
b) What influenced their beliefs?
c) How did this influence affect their actions and the actions of others?

Beliefs expressed in the Negro spirituals

An article published in *The Times* newspaper stated that REM's song 'Everybody hurts' was voted the most depressing song of all time.

It is obvious that the culture around us affects both our emotions and our beliefs.

Discuss:

What do you do to let off steam?

shout | fight | get angry | cry | sing

What would you do to let off steam …?

- If you moan about homework, you get double.
- If you moan about school dinner portions being too small, you get less.
- If you moan about the amount of chores at home, you're given more.
- If you don't tidy your room you are made to sleep in the shed.
- If you shout, scream or moan about any of the above you are beaten.

Slavery

In America during the 18th and 19th centuries many black slaves were treated badly, and they would only be treated worse if they tried to moan about it. If you were a slave you couldn't protest about the way you were treated. If you tried to run away, you could be hunted with dogs and if caught, punished or killed. There was not much hope of improving your situation.

Many slaves sought to let off steam by singing. If the words to the songs were thought to complain about their situation or mock their owners, they would be punished. But they had to raise their spirits somehow. These songs became known as Negro spirituals.

Many slaves were made to go to church, and so many became Christians. Through Christianity they learned of a God who gave them a hope of heaven and paradise when they died. If they didn't have hope in this life, at least they could have hope for the next. Music reminded them of this hope.

Underground railway

100,000 slaves ran away from their masters. In the southern states, escapees would mainly gain freedom in USA's northern states or Canada. They would aim to get across Ohio River. They would hide in people's homes and travel at night, often through rivers, to avoid detection. This became known as the 'underground railway'.

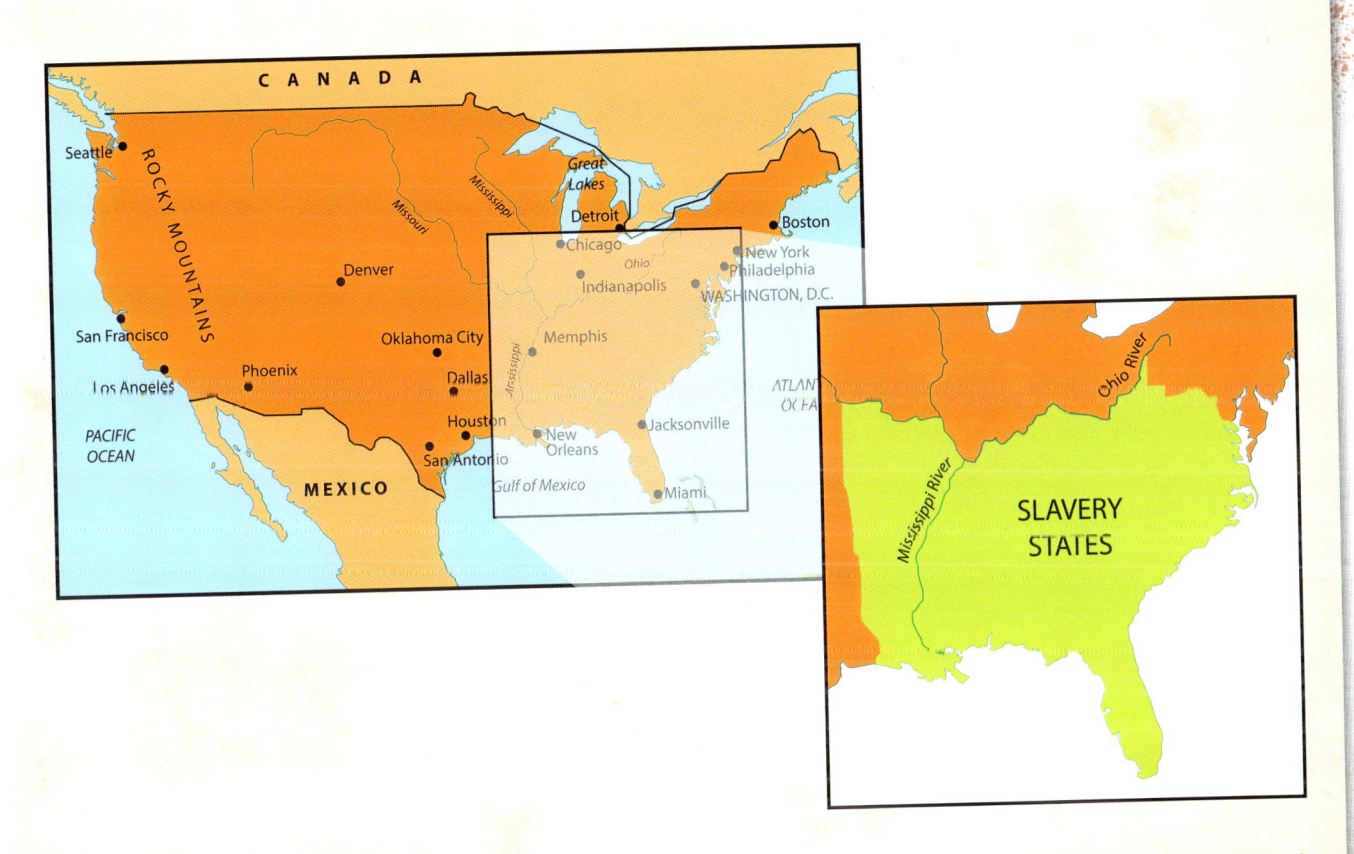

Many Negro spirituals had lyrics (words) that had hidden meanings. The songs had words from the Bible which had a spiritual meaning, but also had another hidden meaning amongst slaves.

ACTIVITY 23

Look at the chart below. On your own version of it, complete the last column.
There are words in the list below that will help you.

Lyrics	Spiritual meaning	Hidden meaning
"free country" "home"	heaven	
"healed" (miracle)	body made well	to gain freedom
"Jordan River"	river where Jesus was baptised	
"Salvation" (saved)	eternal life in heaven	
"railway/station/mainline/chariot"	the journey to heaven	

Word List

Free North   Ohio River   freedom   the 'underground railway'

In the first unit we discussed that beliefs will ultimately affect your actions. So, for example, if you believe that all people are equal, then you might give to charity; if you believe that global warming is due to human action on earth, then you might ensure that lights are turned off when you leave a room.

Culture is made up of the beliefs, actions and interactions of a group of people

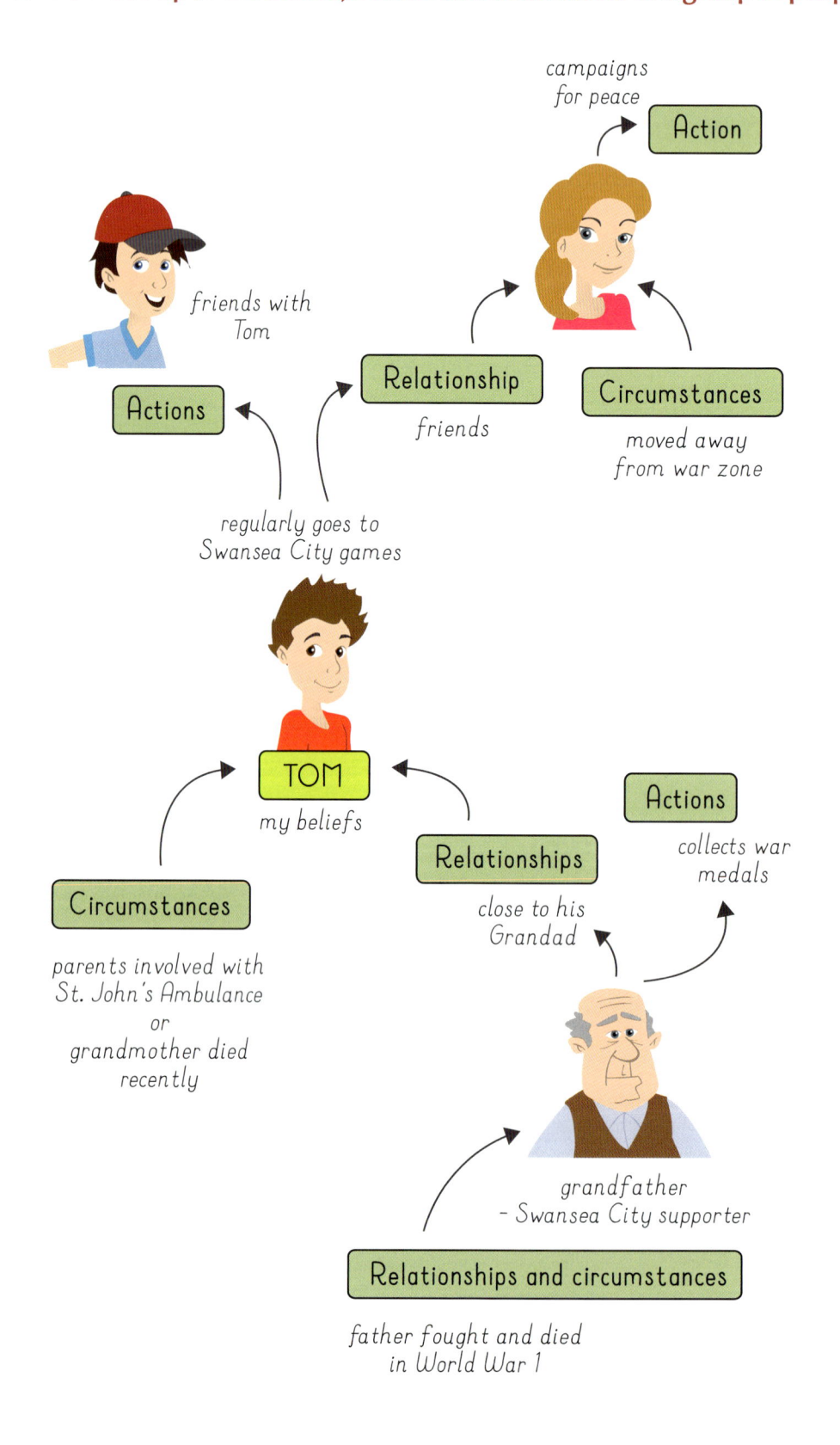

campaigns for peace → **Action**

friends with Tom

Actions ← **Relationship** → **Circumstances**
friends — *moved away from war zone*

regularly goes to Swansea City games

TOM
my beliefs

Circumstances — **Relationships** — **Actions**
parents involved with St. John's Ambulance or grandmother died recently — *close to his Grandad* — *collects war medals*

grandfather - Swansea City supporter

Relationships and circumstances
father fought and died in World War 1

Figure 1

At the beginning of this unit we discussed the concept of culture. Culture is both the influences on a person's life and the actions that influence others.

ACTIVITY 24

a) Have a look at figure 1. Your beliefs are influenced by the events that happen in your life and the people with whom you come into contact. You, in turn, act on those beliefs and influence others. Discuss how this diagram represents culture.

b) Look at the following map, and describe how people in different places in the world demonstrate their culture. This could be through food, music or beliefs.

Cultural origins of religion

There are many religious and non-religious beliefs in Wales today, but each of the main 6 world religions started in a specific place and at a specific time. Find out who started them and when they started.

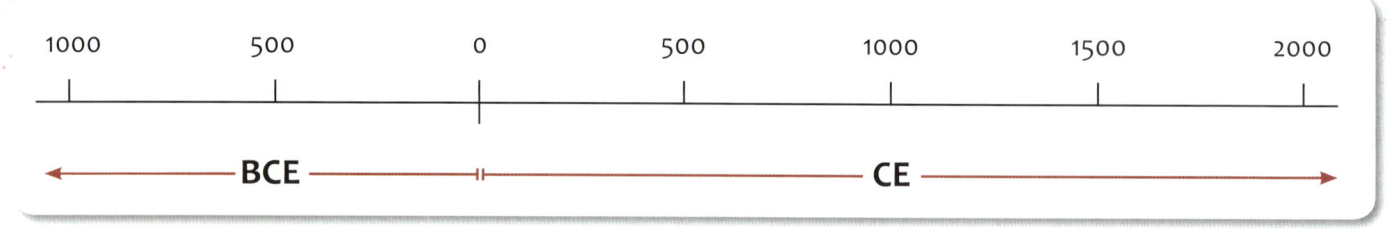

```
1000        500         0         500        1000       1500       2000
 |           |          |          |           |          |          |
←————————— BCE —————————|—————————————————— CE ——————————————————→
```

ACTIVITY 25

a) When and where did the 6 main world religions start? Use the information that follows to complete your own version of the table below.

Religion	Date	Where	Who
Buddhism			
Christianity			
Hinduism			
Islam			
Judaism			
Sikhism			

b) What literacy skills did you use in this exercise?

Christianity

Christianity started around the year 30AD (CE). Jesus, who was born a Jew, started teaching his followers, calling them disciples. Jesus began his ministry in Israel and although he died 3 years after asking the first disciples to follow him, they began to spread his gospel (good news) throughout the then Roman Empire.

Buddhism

A prince named Siddhartha Gautama lived over 2500 years ago. He grew up in a Hindu family in North East India. Siddhartha spent his life trying to find the answer to suffering. Whilst meditating on this question he received the answer and achieved what his followers called 'enlightenment'. From this point on he was known as 'Buddha'. His followers spread this message throughout East Asia.

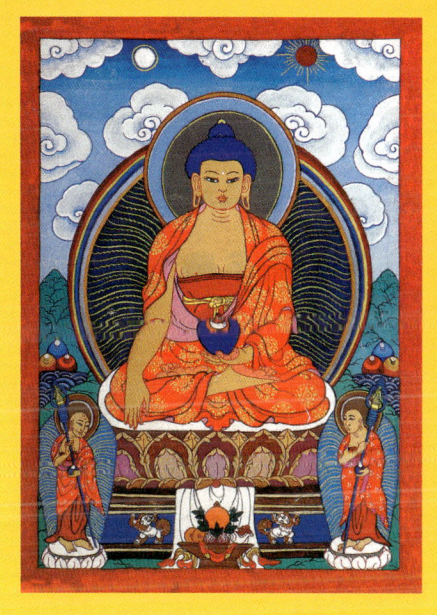

Islam

Muhammad was born in Makkah, around 570 CE in modern day Saudi Arabia. He never knew his father as he had died before Muhammad was born, and his mother passed away when he was only six. When Muhammad was about 40 years old he would take time to think and meditate in the mountains outside Makkah. Whilst meditating in a cave on Mount Hira he began receiving the message of the Qur'an. He began teaching throughout Makkah, gaining followers who continued to spread the message of Islam after his death in 632CE.

Common calligraphic representation of Muhammad's name

Makkah

Hinduism

Hinduism has no founder. It began as the 'culture' or beliefs of a group of people living in the Indus Valley over 4500 years ago. River Indus begins in the Himalayas and flows through the modern day country of Pakistan. Excavations which began over 90 years ago have discovered over 1000 towns and cities in an area bigger than Pakistan itself.

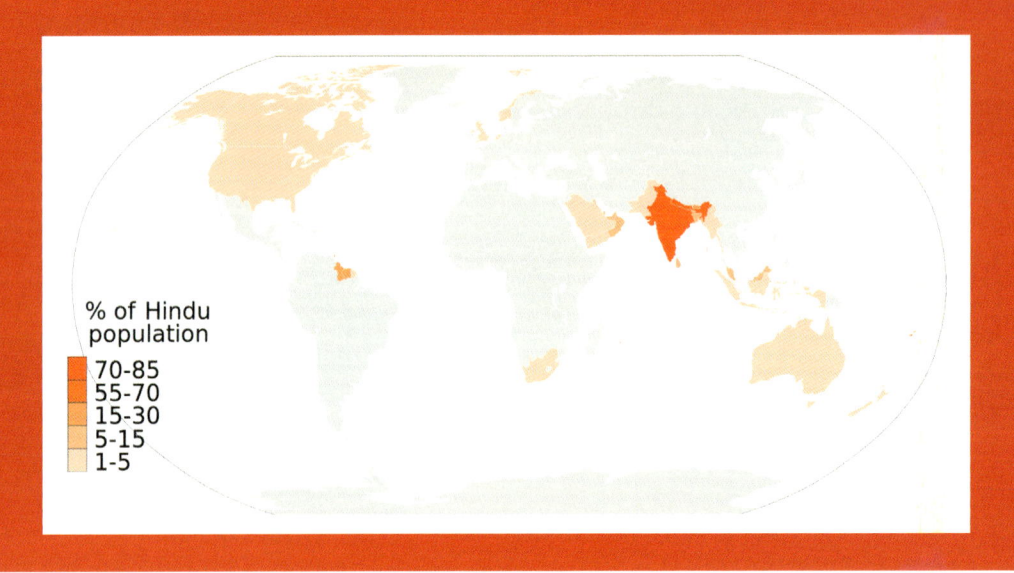

% of Hindu population
- 70-85
- 55-70
- 15-30
- 5-15
- 1-5

Sikhism

Guru Nanak Dev was born to a Hindu family in the Punjab in 1469. As a child, Nanak was very interested in God, gods and religion. It is said that when Nanak was in his thirties he disappeared for 3 days. When he reappeared he explained that he had met with God. He began teaching that people should show devotion to God. He preached that all people were equal, no matter what religion they were. His message spread throughout the region of the Punjab and his followers became known as Sikhs.

Guru Nanak with Bhai Bala and Bhai Mardana and Sikh Gurus

Judaism

Abram was born in Ur, in modern day Iraq, over 4000 years ago. After God changed Abram's name to Abraham He asked him to leave his home and travel west. Abraham travelled to modern day Israel, and although he never actually settled there, his descendants conquered and built the nation of Israel 500 years later.

The bosom of Abraham – medieval illustration from the Hortus deliciarum of Herrad of Landsberg (12th century)

ACTIVITY 26

a) When do you think Islam began? Why?

b) What numeracy skills did you use in a)?

Special places for religious people

Why do you think that many religious people visit places connected to the beginning of their religion? The Bible gives two accounts of where Jesus was born. The **Church of the Nativity** in Bethlehem marks the traditional place of birth.

Luke 2:4-6

⁴ So Joseph also went up from the town of Nazareth in Galilee to Judea, to Bethlehem the town of David, because he belonged to the house and line of David. ⁵ He went there to register with Mary, who was pledged to be married to him and was expecting a child. ⁶ While they were there, the time came for the baby to be born, ⁷ and she gave birth to her firstborn, a son. She wrapped him in cloths and placed him in a manger, because there was no guest room available for them.

(NIV)

Matthew 2:1-6

¹ After Jesus was born in Bethlehem in Judea, during the time of King Herod, Magi from the east came to Jerusalem ² and asked, "Where is the one who has been born king of the Jews? We saw his star when it rose and have come to worship him."

³ When King Herod heard this he was disturbed, and all Jerusalem with him. ⁴ When he had called together all the people's chief priests and teachers of the law, he asked them where the Messiah was to be born. ⁵ "In Bethlehem in Judea," they replied, "for this is what the prophet has written: ⁶ "'But you, Bethlehem, in the land of Judah, are by no means least among the rulers of Judah; for out of you will come a ruler who will be the shepherd my people Israel.'"

(NIV)

Unlike the Bible, the Guru Granth Sahib doesn't contain an account of the Guru Nanak's birth. The founder of Sikhism was born in a village that was originally called Talwindi. The name was changed to Nankana Sahib after he was born. The village has grown to become one of the main cities in its district of the Punjab. Guru Nanak was born on the 15th April 1469 and Sikhs from all over the world visit the city on the anniversary of his birthday. The Gurdwara Janam Asthan was built to mark the birth place of the first Guru.

Read the extract below:

> 'It was amazing just to stand there, to stand where he stood, to see what he saw. I felt so calm, as if he was standing next to me. To experience this next to other people who were seeing and feeling the same things made me really appreciate my faith.'

ACTIVITY 27

Write a blog from the point of view of a pilgrim visiting the birth place of a major world religion.

How do you find out about a person's beliefs?

For many people their beliefs are a part of their culture. You may be able to find out what a person believes about a particular issue based on the way they behave and act. A person may not even know why they believe what they believe. For example, do you believe that the world is round or do you believe that it's flat? How do you know? Have you been to space or sailed around the world? Maybe you believe that the world is round because you've been told by a teacher or seen a photograph of the world from space.

It is not always easy to know what a person believes.

ACTIVITY 28

a) Suppose the following photographs have been taken out of 3 different autobiographies. What assumptions can we make about the people in these photographs?

b) Read the descriptions relating to the photographs (see page 48). How accurate were your assumptions?

The phrase 'You can't judge a book by its cover' means you can't jump to conclusions on the grounds of a little information. Photographs only tell part of the story, but with a little explanation they make a lot more sense.

38

ACTIVITY 29

a) Look at the photographs of the people below. What do you know about their beliefs?

b) Where could you find out more about what they believe?

Many cultures have literature that gives an insight into the beliefs and practices at that time. The Black Book of Carmarthen is one of Wales' oldest books. Although it was written around 1250CE, it contains poems that relate to events that took place hundreds of years before. It contains references to King Arthur and Myrddin (Merlin). Although the book is kept at the National Library of Wales in Aberystwyth, there is a digital version available for all to see on-line.

All of the 6 main world religions have books and literature that they consider sacred. Many of the books have information that is important when considering the beliefs of that religion.

ACTIVITY 30

Read the descriptions below, and check which of the statements on page 49 are true and which are false.

The Bible

The Bible is a collection of 66 books that are important to Christians. Some Christians think that the Bible contains a clear message from God to humanity. Others think that it is a collection of writings and stories that contain moral teaching. The Bible is made up of 66 separate books written by over 40 different people over a period of 1500 years. The 39 books of the Old Testament describe the period from creation to about 400BCE. The Old Testament includes the history of the Jewish people, including the 10 Commandments. There are 27 books in the New Testament. The New Testament starts with the events leading up to the birth of Jesus and the parables that he used to teach important messages.

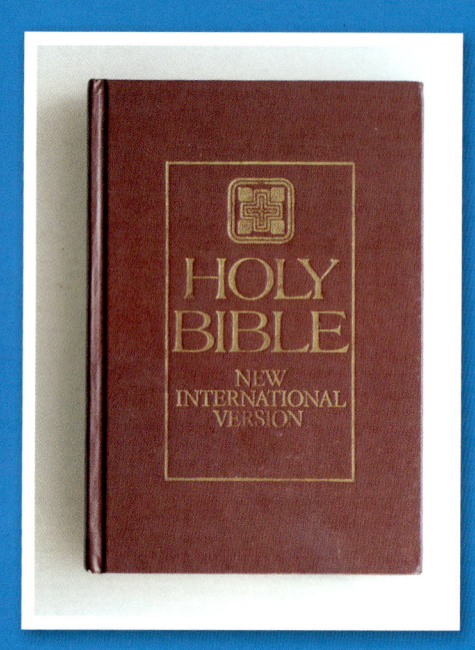

The Qur'an

The Qur'an is the holy book of Muslims. It was written in Arabic and is a collection of messages received by Muhammad over a period of 20 years. Muslims believe that the words in the Qur'an are the words of Allah given to Muhammad by the Angel Jibril in the 6th and 7th century CE. Many Muslims learn Arabic so that they can understand the Qur'an in its original language. Those who memorise all 114 chapters (or *surahs*) of the Qur'an are called *Hafiz*. The Qur'an is usually kept on the highest shelf in a Muslim's home and it will never be put on the floor. Many Muslims will place it on a special stand and wash before reading it.

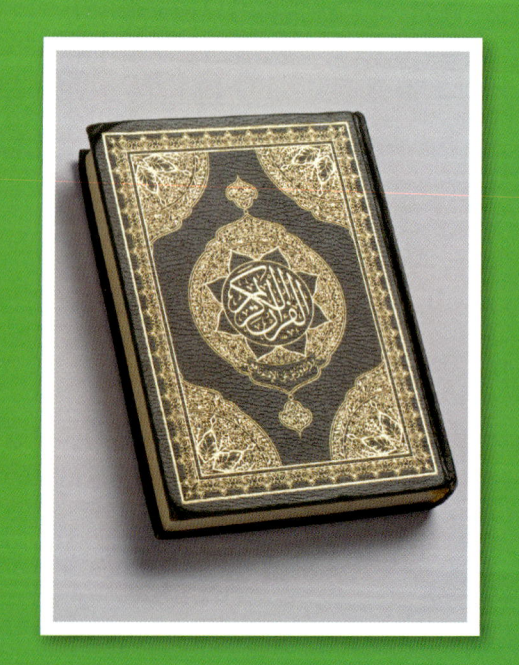

The Guru Granth Sahib

The Guru Granth Sahib is the holy book of Sikhs. It contains many Hindu and Sikh hymns. It was created by the 10th Guru, Guru Gobind Singh, before he died in 1708. 'Guru' means 'teacher' and the book is the 11th and final Guru. A building that contains a Guru Granth Sahib is called a *gurdwara*. The book is treated with the same respect as a Guru would expect. Sikhs never turn their back on it and it is never placed on the floor. Every evening a Guru Granth Sahib is 'put to bed', by covering it in silk cloth, and each morning it is placed on a special platform called a *Manji Sahib*.

The Torah

The Torah, or the 'Five Books of Moses', explains what many Jews believe happened at the beginning of creation. It also explains how the Jews were made to work as slaves in Egypt, how God heard their cries and used Moses to free the people. It contains 613 laws, including the 10 Commandments. In a Jewish synagogue the Torah is found in the form of a scroll. It is kept in a special place called 'the ark', right at the front of the synagogue's main hall. The Torah is part of a bigger book called the Tanach. The Tanach contains many of the writings that are in the Christian Bible's Old Testament.

The Tripitaka/Tipitaka

The Tripitaka is the oldest collection of Buddhist teachings. It was written in the Pāli language, so the book is also called the Pāli Canon. There are over 40 volumes divided into three main sections; the first section contains a set of 227 rules for Buddhist monks, the second describes the life of the Buddha, and the third section explains the Buddha's teachings. 'Tripitaka' means 'three baskets' and probably refers to the way the writings were first stored.

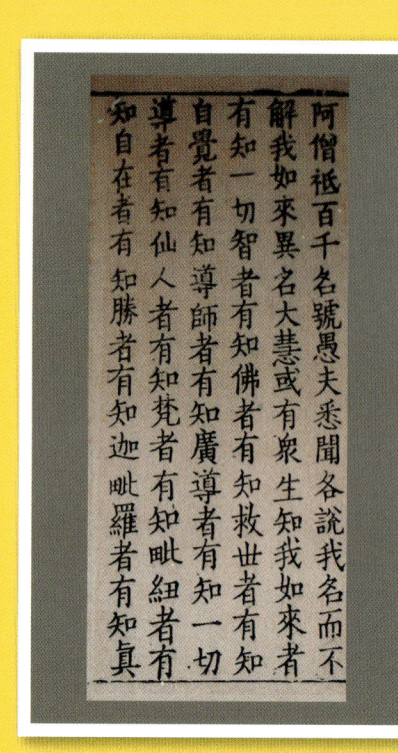

The Hindu Vedas

The Vedas are four important collections of writings that are important to Hindus. They were originally written in ancient Sanskrit. The Vedas contain hymns, beliefs and rituals from the people of the Indus Valley, and date back to 1500BCE. The Vedas are some of the oldest religious writings still around today. They contain stories of the Hindu gods and explain how the world started. They also have information about the everyday life of the people living in India three to four thousand years ago.

Influence

When you want to find out about a person's beliefs, it is important to know what to ask and where to look. Knowing whether a person follows the teachings of a particular holy book will help you to understand what a person believes about a wide range of issues.

ACTIVITY 31

Read the following passages and explain the effect it may have on a religious person.

Bible
For since we believe that Jesus died and was raised to life again, we also believe that when Jesus returns, God will bring back with him the believers who have died. (1 Thessalonians 4:14)

Qur'an
Ramadan is the (month) in which the Qur'an was sent down, as a guide to mankind and a clear guidance and judgment (so that mankind will distinguish from right and wrong)... (Qur'an 2:183)
Oh you who believe! Fasting is prescribed to you as it was prescribed to those before you, that you may learn piety and righteousness. (Qur'an 2:183)

Guru Granth Sahib
They are not said to be husband and wife, who merely sit together. Rather they alone are called husband and wife, who have one soul in two bodies.

Vedas
Charity gives a deep sense of self-satisfaction. (Rig Veda)

Tripitaka
To stop suffering, stop greediness. Greediness is a source of suffering.

Torah
⁴ You shall not make for yourself an image in the form of anything in heaven above or on the earth beneath or in the waters below. ⁵ You shall not bow down to them or worship them; for I, the LORD your God, am a jealous God, punishing the children for the sin of the parents to the third and fourth generation of those who hate me, ⁶ but showing love to a thousand generations of those who love me and keep my commandments. (Exodus 20:4)

As well as the main books that we have looked at, there are also other books that include teachings from the founders or other important figures. Religious writings and books are an important source of information for any believer. But just because it is written in a holy book doesn't necessarily mean that a religious person will believe it. For example, many differences in Christianity are owing to how individual Christians interpret particular parts of the Bible.

ACTIVITY 32

Find out some key differences for people within the same religion, e.g. Christian: Catholic and Protestant; Muslim: Sunni and Shia; Buddhism: Theravada and Mahayana.

The following questions will help you:
- What are the key differences?
- Why are they there?
- How do they affect their actions?

How do beliefs affect heritage and culture?

Although each religion started in a particular place in the world and at a particular time, it is clear that the beliefs spread. The distance between Cardiff (Wales) and Jerusalem (Israel) is 2367 miles, but there is evidence that Christians live in Cardiff. What evidence is there that religious people live in your town?

Cardiff

Jerusalem

Cardiff

Jerusalem

ACTIVITY 33

Look at the following data.

What evidence is there that religion is important in Cardiff?

Table 6a
religion by local authority in Wales, 2011

Local Authority	All residents	Christian		Buddhist	
	persons	persons	percentage	persons	percentage
Isle of Anglesey	69,751	45,400	65.1	165	0.2
Gwynedd	121,874	72,503	59.5	426	0.3
Conwy	115,228	74,506	64.7	347	0.3
Denbighshire	93,734	60,129	64.1	266	0.3
Flintshire	152,506	101,298	66.4	344	0.2
Wrexham	134,844	85,576	63.5	351	0.3
Powys	132,976	82,120	61.8	567	0.4
Ceredigion	75,922	43,981	57.9	355	0.5
Pembrokeshire	122,439	77,162	63.0	422	0.3
Carmarthenshire	183,777	113,534	61.8	420	0.2
Swansea	239,023	131,451	55.0	856	0.4
Neath Port Talbot	139,812	80,646	57.7	312	0.2
Bridgend	139,178	76,625	55.1	357	0.3
The Vale of Glamorgan	126,336	73,384	58.1	356	0.3
Cardiff	346,090	177,743	51.4	1,690	0.5
Rhondda Cynon Taf	234,410	118,388	50.5	518	0.2
Merthyr Tydfil	58,802	32,948	56.0	124	0.2
Caerphilly	178,806	90,669	50.7	278	0.2
Blaenau Gwent	69,814	34,805	49.9	112	0.2
Torfaen	91,075	50,472	55.4	222	0.2
Monmouthshire	91,323	57,101	62.5	269	0.3
Newport	145,736	82,858	56.9	360	0.2
Wales	3,063,456	1,763,299	57.6	9,117	0.3

continued

Table 6b
religion by local authority in Wales, 2011

local authority	Hindu		Jewish		Muslim	
	persons	percentage	persons	percentage	persons	percentage
Isle of Anglesey	45	0.1	40	0.1	250	0.4
Gwynedd	238	0.2	55	0.0	1,378	1.1
Conwy	206	0.2	62	0.1	583	0.5
Denbighshire	167	0.2	32	0.0	469	0.5
Flintshire	158	0.1	70	0.0	482	0.3
Wrexham	504	0.4	58	0.0	860	0.6
Powys	324	0.2	80	0.1	235	0.2
Ceredigion	197	0.3	64	0.1	521	0.7
Pembrokeshire	230	0.2	50	0.0	425	0.3
Carmarthenshire	351	0.2	82	0.0	625	0.3
Swansea	780	0.3	159	0.1	5,415	2.3
Neath Port Talbot	144	0.1	39	0.0	573	0.4
Bridgend	270	0.2	33	0.0	529	0.4
The Vale of Glamorgan	269	0.2	90	0.1	785	0.6
Cardiff	1,700	1.4	802	0.2	23,656	6.8
Rhondda Cynon Taf	401	0.2	87	0.0	1,061	0.5
Merthyr Tydfil	80	0.1	4	0.0	197	0.3
Caerphilly	174	0.1	69	0.0	391	0.2
Blaenau Gwent	72	0.1	8	0.0	179	0.3
Torfaen	241	0.3	16	0.0	238	0.3
Monmouthshire	162	0.2	65	0.1	239	0.3
Newport	685	0.5	99	0.1	6,859	4.7
Wales	10,434	0.3	2,064	0.1	45,950	1.5

continued

2011 Census: First Results for Ethnicity, National Identity, and Religion for Wales (Welsh Government)

ACTIVITY 34

Look at the map of Cardiff below. How many references to religion can you see in the map?

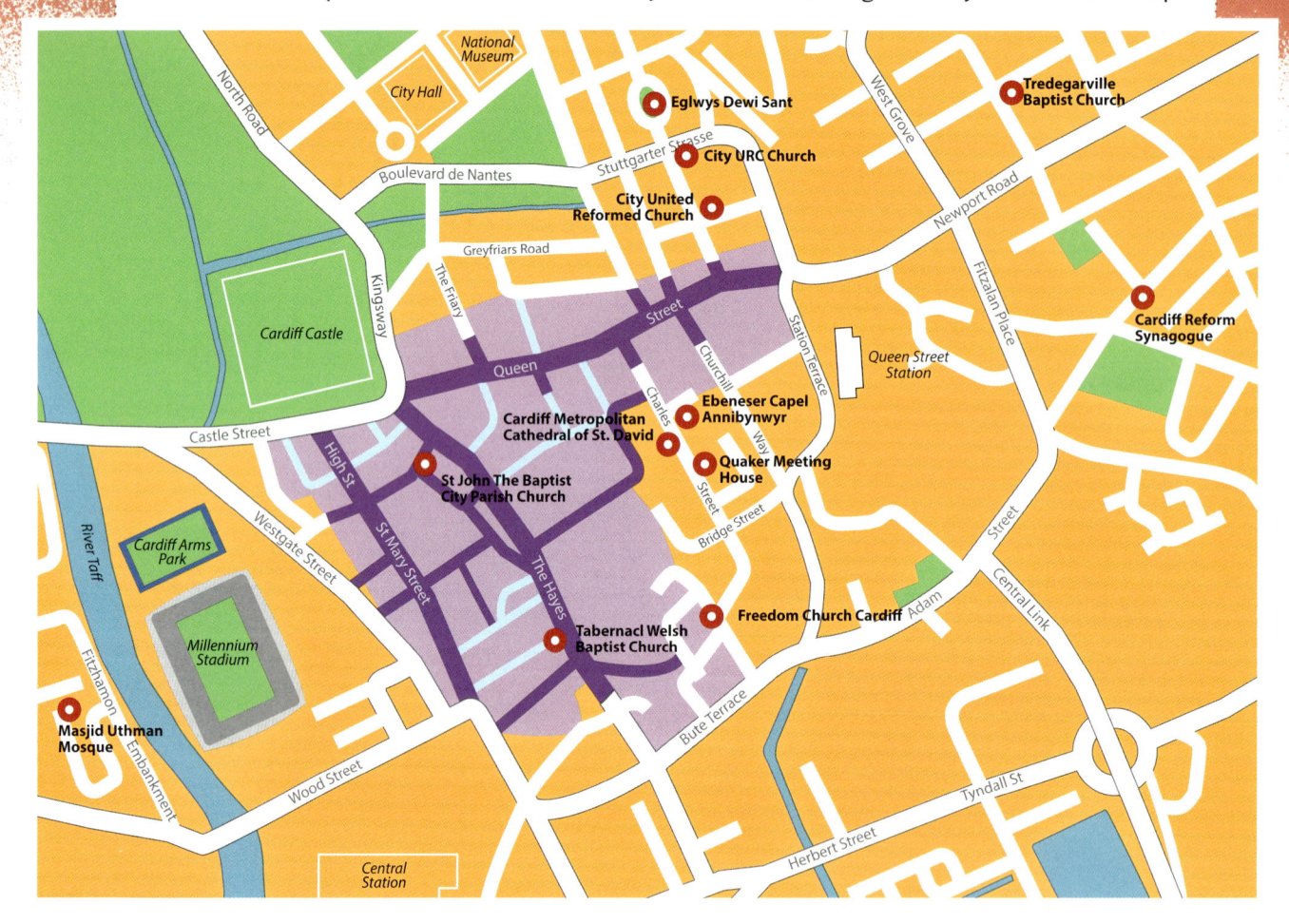

Religion has clearly had an impact on Wales. The physical evidence of large cathedral cities, parish churches and chapels and other religious buildings show that religion is practised today. There are ruins of religious buildings all over Wales, like Valle Crucis Abbey in Llangollen and Basingwerk Abbey in Flintshire. These buildings demonstrate that Christianity has been important in Wales' past. Many countries in the world will have evidence that religions play an important part in the life of its people.

In this unit we have discussed the impact that culture has on beliefs. It is clear that religion has had an impact on the landscape and it has also had an impact on our celebrations, but for many people religion has a far more important impact – it affects the way they understand their place in the world.

For 3 of the 6 world religions, each person's life on earth has a clear beginning and a definite end. Generally, Jews, Christians and Muslims believe that we only have one chance to live our life and that the choices that we make will affect what happens to us after we die. If we make the correct choices, we live on in some form of paradise/heaven, if not, we receive punishment, possibly in hell.

Hinduism, Buddhism and Sikhism have a very different view about life. Rather than it being seen as a straight line with a clear beginning and an end, life is more like a circle. Reincarnation means that a person is born again after they die. The law of Karma means that if you are good in this life you are born again as something better, but if you are bad you will be born again as something worse. The aim of living each life is to be born again as something better until your soul is released from this world and enters a form of paradise.

To highlight the similarities between the two groups of religions, Judaism, Christianity and Islam are often referred to as the Western religions. Sometimes they are called the Abrahamic religions, because they all consider Abraham as an important person. Hinduism, Buddhism and Sikhism are called the Eastern religions.

ACTIVITY 35

Match the words below with the numbers in the diagram to help describe Eastern beliefs and Western beliefs about life and death.

- Heaven/paradise
- Hinduism
- Karma (the good or bad choices and actions in life)
- Re-birth
- Islam
- Sikhism
- Birth
- Paradise
- Life
- Death
- Buddhism
- Judaism
- Hell/Punishment
- Birth
- Christianity

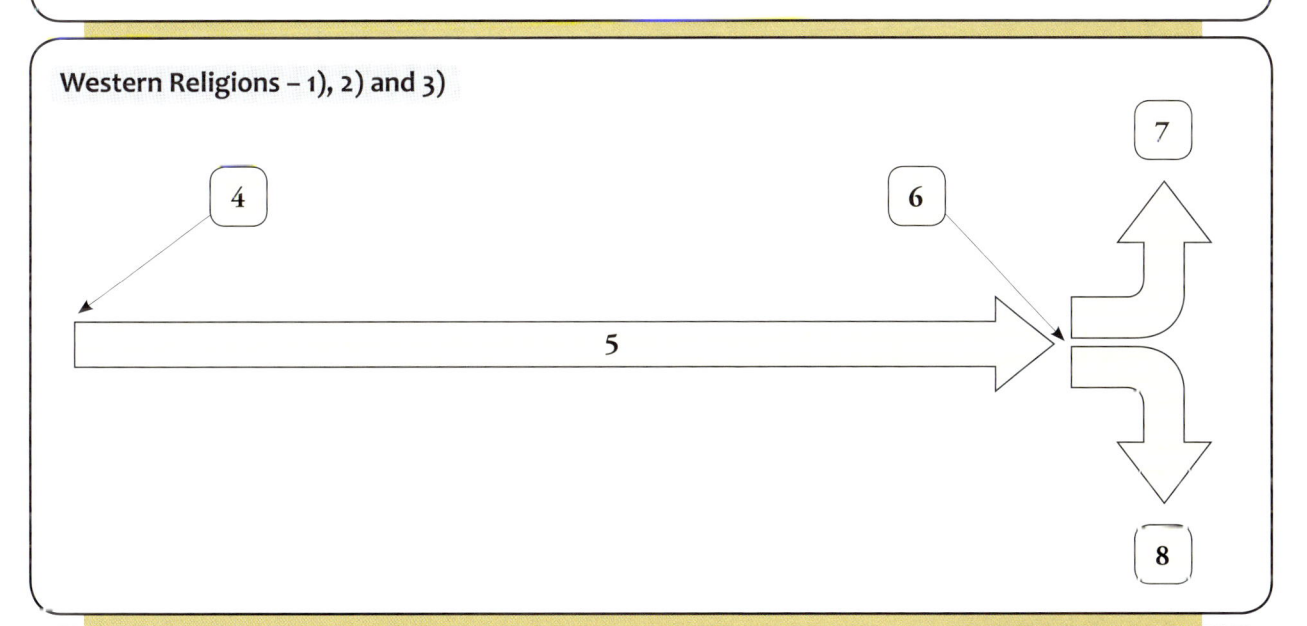

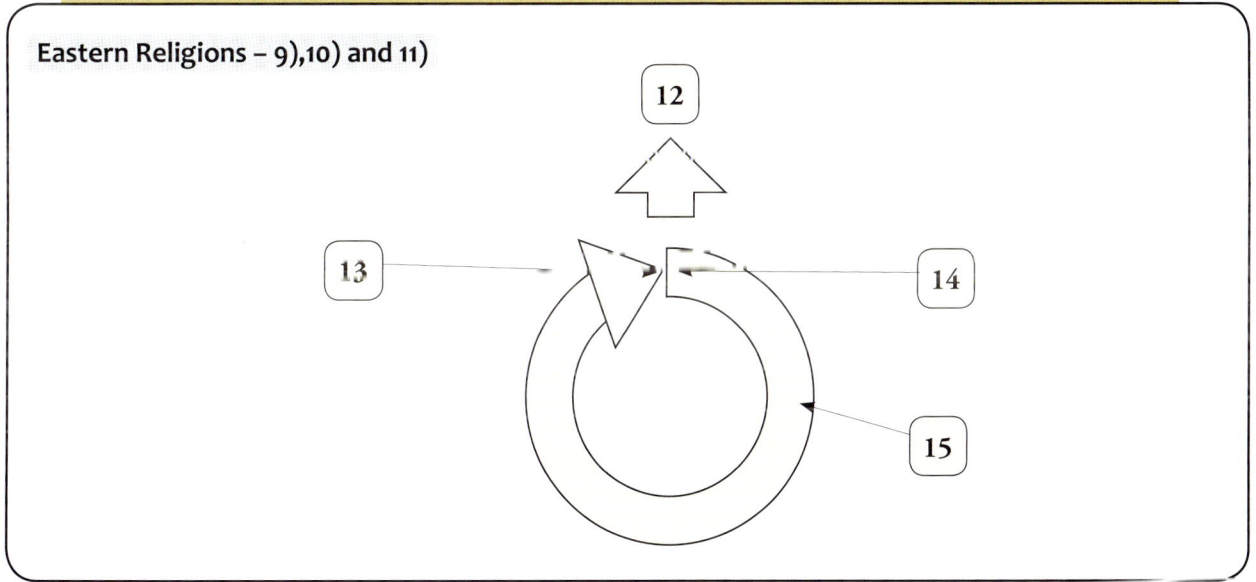

Western Religions – 1), 2) and 3)

4, 5, 6, 7, 8

Eastern Religions – 9), 10) and 11)

12, 13, 14, 15

Summing up: Does my culture define me?

In this unit we have considered who affects our beliefs, from family and friends to people we may have never met, through their song lyrics or their books. It is important to remember the culture that we live in and the effect it has on what we think and do.

We have explored the beginnings of each of the 6 main world religions. People are connected to the past, and learning about how a religion or culture started may help to understand the types of things that are important to a group of people.

By looking at the various holy books, we are able to find out why people believe the things they do and, more importantly, act and behave in the way they do.

Most importantly, we must try to understand that the collected beliefs of the people around us shape the culture we live in. The culture we live in helps to shape the beliefs we have.

Supporting information

ACTIVITY 28 (page 38)

1. 'We were on holiday in Mallorca and my wife and I were walking along the marina in Palma. We stopped to admire a sailboat and started chatting to the owner. It turned out that he had family in our town back home and he offered to take us out into the bay on the sailboat. He took this photograph of my wife and me pretending to steer the boat!'

2. 'It was my 40th birthday. I walked down the stairs and my children were sitting in the lounge waiting, surrounded by balloons. They gave me a large picture frame covered in colourful wrapping paper. As I began to open the present I saw my face on the body of a fireman walking away from a fire. "Fantastic!" I exclaimed as Tomos, my eighteen year old, began to explain how he'd used photoshop and an old photo of me. The photograph has taken pride of place in my surgery.'

3. 'I was at the end of my tether! My wife had left me and I was struggling to pay the rent. I visited the job centre daily, but there was nothing for an unemployed builder. I borrowed a clown outfit from a mate and advertised myself as an entertainer for children's parties.'

ACTIVITY 30 (p40-42)

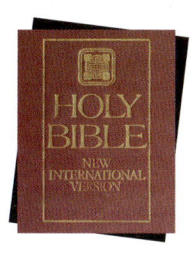

The Bible

True or false

1. The Bible is made up of 66 different books.
2. The Bible was written by one person.
3. The Bible was written over a period of 1500 years.
4. There are 39 books of the Old Testament covering the period from creation to the end of the world.
5. Many of Jesus' teachings were taught using stories called parables.

The Qur'an

True or false

1. The Qur'an is the written message that was given to Muhammad, through the angel Jibril, by Allah.
2. Chapters in the Qur'an are called *surahs*.
3. The Qur'an is made up of 112 *surahs*.
4. The Qur'an should only be read in English.
5. A person who memorises the whole of the Qur'an is called a *Hafiz*.

The Guru Granth Sahib

True or false

1. The Sikh holy book is the 9th Guru/teacher of Sikhism.
2. Each Guru Granth Sahib is well looked after and is 'put to bed' every night.
3. A building that contains a Guru Granth Sahib is called a *gurdwara*.
4. The Guru Granth Sahib is made up only of Sikh hymns collected together by Guru Gobind Singh.
5. The Guru Granth Sahib is kept on the floor.

The Torah

True or false

1. The Torah is also called the '5 books of Abraham'.
2. The Torah is usually a scroll.
3. The Torah is part of a bigger collection of books called the Old Testament.
4. The Torah contains over 613 laws.
5. In a synagogue the Torah is kept in a special place called the ark.

The Tripitaka

True or false

1. It is also called the Pāli Canon, after the person who wrote it.
2. The word 'Tripitaka' means 'three sections'.
3. A section of the Tripitaka contains 227 rules for Buddhist monks.
4. The life of the Buddha is described in the Tripitaka.
5. The teachings of the Buddha can be found in the Tripitaka.

The Hindu Vedas

True or false

1. There are 5 Vedas.
2. The Vedas only contain information about the Hindu religion.
3. They date back to 1500BCE.
4. The Vedas explain how the world began.
5. The Vedas are some of the oldest religious writings still around today.

UNIT 3
DOES FAITH STAND THE TEST?

Engage with fundamental questions:

Does faith really matter anyway?

Why are the beliefs and views of others found threatening?

Is there any proof that faith is valuable in life?

Explore Beliefs,

- Who or what people believe in.
- How beliefs are so important in people's lives.
- How people respond when their beliefs are questioned or denied.

Teachings

- Jewish, Christian, Muslim and Buddhist teachings about believing and faith.
- 2 sacred stories from Judaism and Christianity.

and Practices

- Muslim practices in daily life.
- Responses to persecution and oppression.

Express:

Using your own opinions along with what you have found out …

Why is faith so important to some people?

How does faith help people when under pressure?

Can faith endure any situation or circumstance?

Who and what affects my belief?

Do some people lose their faith? Why?

My faith matters to me

In whatever way a person's beliefs are shaped and nurtured, their faith usually matters to them a lot. Because beliefs shape the way we look at life and the way we respond to it, they matter to us. None of us like it when our beliefs are dismissed, ridiculed or questioned by others. The values and principles which are at the centre of all that we are and do, are precious, and most of us will not give them up without a struggle.

One of the most well known stories of a person who refuses to give up his faith is that of Job, in the Bible. Here is a simple poetic version of the story:

Out of the whirlwind

Job was a good man doing his best.
Happy with life he was truly blessed.
All his ten children, whom he adored
Seemed to be part of God's reward.

But then it all changed to a living hell
As one by one disasters fell.
He lost his home, his children died,
All trace of happiness was denied.

Illness struck bringing endless pain.
He was tested over and over again.
He tried to keep faith and hold his nerve
In the face of suffering he didn't deserve.

He even blamed God, speaking out in prayer
That his life he could no longer bear.
Then while he was calling upon God's name
Out of the whirlwind an answer came.
'It's not for you to question why,
For I am the creator of land and sky.'

The words seemed hard from the voice that replied.
But it showed God was listening, and by his side.
Job's life was restored, there was no more pain.
He found a new family and was happy again.

He now could accept what God tried to show
That His purpose and power are too great to know,
But whatever the suffering, God always would
Help people come through it and use it for good.

ACTIVITY 36

Look below at the ways Job's faith was tested. Select the one you think would be the hardest to have faced, and give a reason for your choice.

Then ask for the list of outcomes for Job because of his faith. Now explain why Job's faith mattered to him, and what was the benefit of keeping his faith.

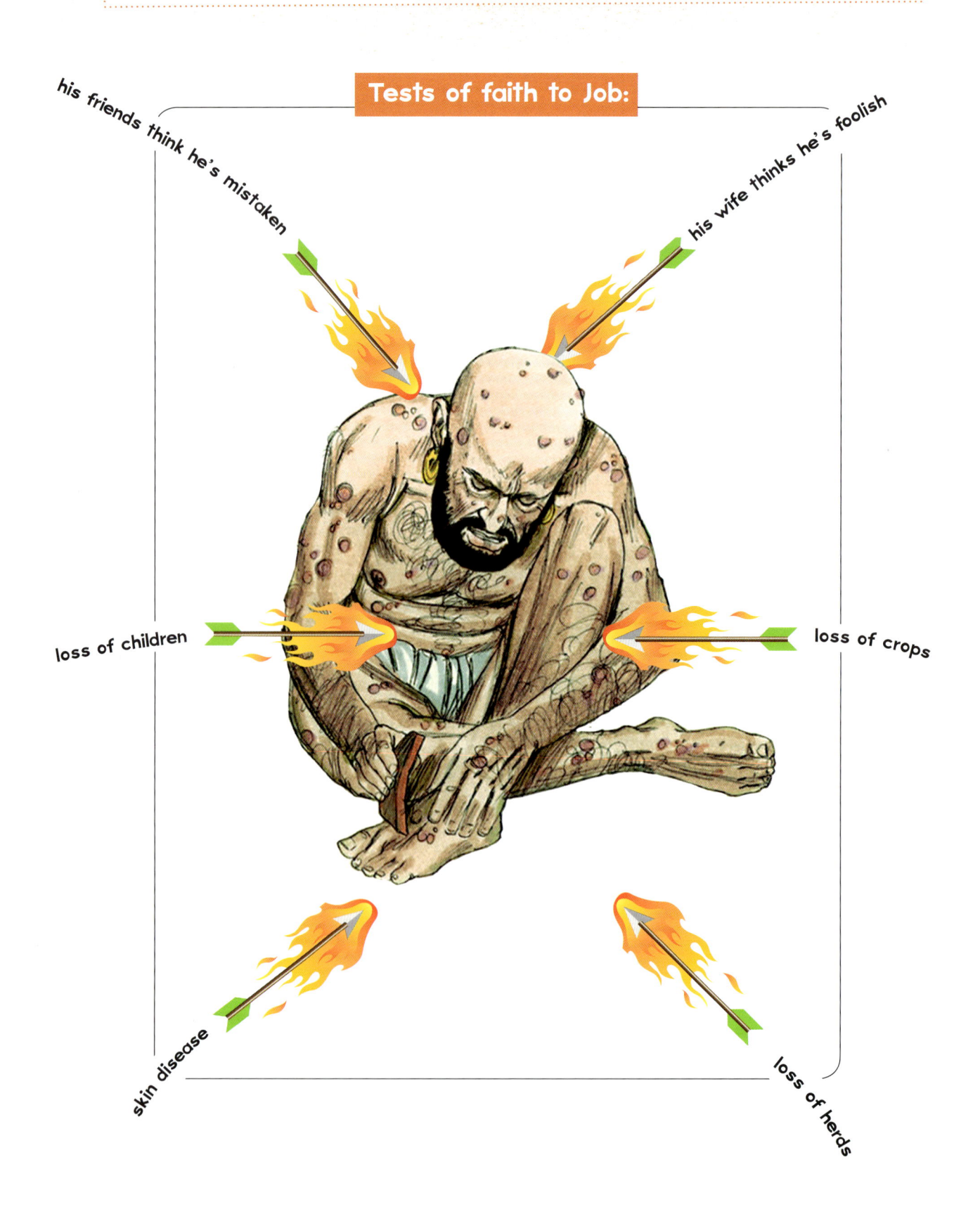

Tests of faith to Job:

- his friends think he's mistaken
- his wife thinks he's foolish
- loss of children
- loss of crops
- skin disease
- loss of herds

52

When faith in God matters to people, like it did to Job, then they always see that there are positive outcomes to hanging on to that faith, and trusting in the God in whom they have believed.

If culture helps to shape the beliefs we have, then the next question to ask is 'How do our beliefs stand the test of the experiences and challenges in life?'

It is quite normal to experience times of testing and hardship in life. Everyone has times when things are difficult and demanding, and it seems then that everything goes wrong or becomes more difficult.

ACTIVITY 37

Think about a time when you found things really difficult - whether in school or in family life. Try to think of the emotions you had during those difficult days. Write down the different emotions you had and give them a score out of 5, 1 being 'noticeable' and 5 being 'severe'.

Now try to think back and consider how you coped during that time. What gave you strength? What helped you? Which people were helpful, and how? Try and note some of these down on a piece of paper, if you can, and keep it somewhere safe.

These will be private to you alone. No one is going to look at them, unless you want them to do so.

People who are religious are no different from anyone else, except that they have religious beliefs. They also experience the same difficulties in life, and sometimes they will have additional difficulties because of their religious beliefs.

For example, Muslims are told that they should:

- avoid alcohol and other mind altering drugs
- believe that there is only one God and that Muhammad is his prophet, or messenger
- give to charity, and help those in need
- pray five times a day every day
- dress modestly
- fast during the hours of daylight during Ramadan
- go to Makkah at least once in their lifetime

ACTIVITY 38

Look at each of the requirements for Muslims on Page 54, and describe what you think (a) would be the difficulties of doing each thing, (b) how each thing might really test personal faith, having to do them in a culture and country that does not easily fit in with them, and (c) how personal religious faith might actually help believers to keep these requirements.

There are many ways in which a person's faith can be tested. Below is a list of possible things. Read through them all, and try to empathise with a person who is experiencing them.

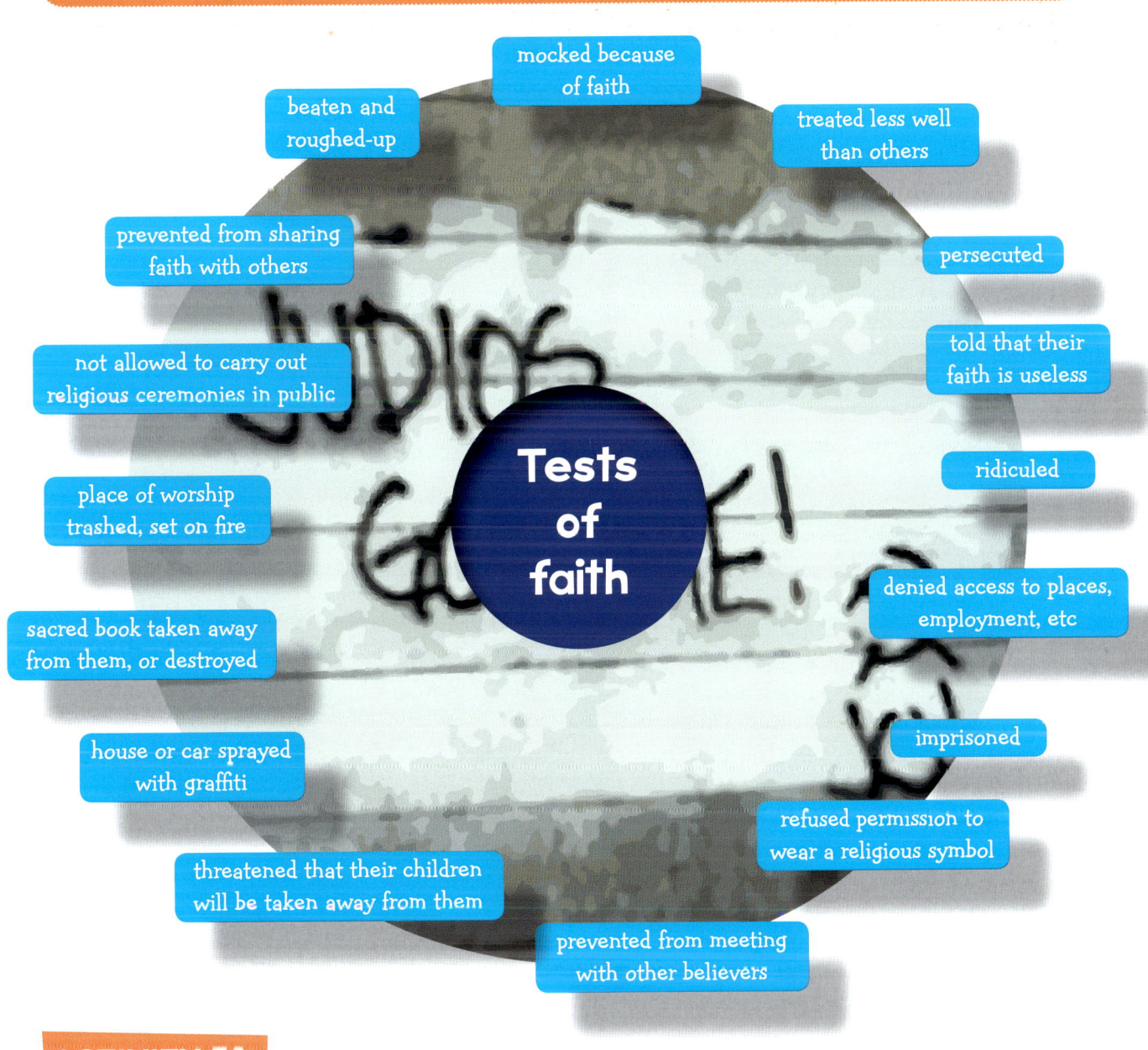

Tests of faith

- mocked because of faith
- beaten and roughed-up
- treated less well than others
- prevented from sharing faith with others
- persecuted
- not allowed to carry out religious ceremonies in public
- told that their faith is useless
- ridiculed
- place of worship trashed, set on fire
- denied access to places, employment, etc
- sacred book taken away from them, or destroyed
- house or car sprayed with graffiti
- imprisoned
- refused permission to wear a religious symbol
- threatened that their children will be taken away from them
- prevented from meeting with other believers

ACTIVITY 39

(a) Having thought about and empathised with people who are experiencing these tests of their faith, complete an analysis of any three of them, describing (i) the effect of each on the person (and on their family), (ii) how each might help to strengthen their faith, and (iii) the effects, positive and negative, on the community.

(b) Choose one of your three, and try to produce a piece of artwork that shows visually the three descriptions for it.

How people react when their faith is tested can vary greatly. Some people fear others around them, and so quickly give up their faith, and try to relate to the thoughts and beliefs of those with whom they associate. Others decide that their faith matters to them, but if other people are not happy with it, then they should practise it on their own, quietly and personally. Others feel that faith is so important, and is about something so completely true, that they must live it out – whatever the consequences.

There is a parable of Jesus in the New Testament that illustrates this idea.

"There once was a man planting seeds in his field. Some seeds fell beside the road. The birds came and ate them up.
Other seeds fell on rocky ground, where there was not much soil. Those seeds sprouted up easily enough. Because there was nowhere for their roots to find water, though, they died as soon as it became hot.
Some seed fell among the thistles. The weeds choked the grain plants.
Other seeds fell on good soil. These plants grew strong and tall. The fruit they grew was thirty to a hundred times more than what was first planted.

Jesus looked at all the people listening. A few nodded. They understood. But many more were shaking their heads. They did not know what Jesus was talking about. So Jesus explained the story:
'The seeds are the lessons I teach. Some people hear the word of God. Sometimes they choose to ignore what they have heard. Then God's enemy, like the birds in the story, steals away what little truth they did manage to learn. These are like the seeds planted by the roadside.
The seeds planted in rocky places are the people who hear with joy what I teach. They try for a little while to follow me. It does not take much, just a few problems, before they go back to their old ways.
The seeds sown with the thistles are the people who hear the word. They also know what I've taught. But then they let the problems of daily living choke the new life.
They worry and want to make more money. So nothing comes from the lessons learned.
Lastly, there are the seeds which are planted on good ground. They are the people who listen and practise what they have learned from my stories. They tell God that they are sorry for what they have done. They try their hardest to change. These people will teach others about following me. They will teach by saying, as well as doing."

ACTIVITY 40

Work in pairs, sitting back to back. One person will have a blank card, the other a card with a simple image. The person with the image is to give instructions about how to draw the image – without actually mentioning what it is. There will be a time limit for the activity.

When the time is up, compare the images. Answer the following questions:
- How many found it really difficult to describe the image?
- How many found it difficult to understand what you were being told?
- How many were really frustrated while trying to do the task?
- How many just gave up, or where tempted to do so?
- How many managed to get a fairly close copy of the original?

In a very simple way, what you have just done, and the difficulties and frustrations you felt, are a bit like the parable that Jesus told. Some people found it easy to understand at first, but then difficult to keep going; others did manage it, and succeeded.

Exercising faith, especially when it is being tested and tried, is a bit like that.
In some parts of the world, people are not always free to live out their religious faith, despite the Universal Declaration of Human Rights.

For example, the Maldives is the only country in the world that requires by law all its citizens to be Muslim. It is a beautiful place, and very popular with tourists from all over the world, but few realise that it is a place that does not allow any freedom of religion or religious thought and practice at all.

There are no churches, and no non-Islamic religious gatherings can take place. The authorities ensure that there is no deviation from Islam.

Another country where it is extremely hard to be a member of any world religion is North Korea. It is a communist state and strongly opposes religion of any kind. If you practise a religion, you are classed as hostile, and face arrest, detention and torture – even public execution. A system of labour camps punishes religious believers with hard work, severe conditions, and extreme political and 'thought' training. Here is the story of one Christian woman who was imprisoned in one of those camps:

Hea Woo (*) is a Christian from North Korea. She was arrested because she was a Christian and was trying to escape to China. She was sent to a labour camp. This is her own story:

"When I arrived at the camp I was shocked by the sign on the gate.
It said, "DO NOT TRY TO ESCAPE, YOU WILL BE KILLED".
Every day in the camp was like torture.
We had to get up at five o'clock.
First, the guards counted us.
We received only a few spoons of rice at breakfast.
Then we had to walk outside of the camp to work on the land.

When we were finally done, there was a criticism session in the camp, where you had to explain what you did wrong that day, and accuse others too.
After we ate a little, there was a long session of ideological training.
It was so hard to keep awake!
At ten we finally could go to bed.

I often felt afraid and alone in the camp.
I prayed to God that He help me to survive.
I prayed for the opportunity one day to tell my story about the camp, and God's work in North Korea.

When people died, the guards burned the corpses and scattered the ashes over the road. We walked that road every day, and each time I thought, 'One day the other prisoners will walk over me'.

I meditated on Psalm 23 every day.
Even though I was in the valley of the shadow of death, I did not fear anything.
God comforted me every day.
God gave me the strength to help other prisoners.
I shared my food with sick people, and I helped to wash their clothes.
God even encouraged me to tell some prisoners about Him.
Five people came to faith, and we had secret meetings in toilets and other hidden places.
They were on the edge of death, and I could give them a message of hope.
All of us survived the camp because we helped each other.

After a few years in the camp I was released.
When the gate opened I ran through it and I did not stop running.
Not once did I look back!
God had heard my prayers.

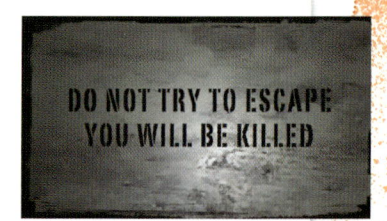

*"He helped me to escape to South Korea.
For the first time in my life I experienced the freedom to do what I want, to believe and to live.*

*My life has been very hard, but Jesus is always watching over me.
Thanks to Open Doors, I can now tell my story.
Please pray for the prisoners in North Korea, and the Christians who are not free to worship, and risk their lives every day."*

(*) Hea Woo is not her real name, as her identity needs to be protected, for her own safety.

Hea Woo's story used with permission of Open Doors UK & Ireland, a charity serving persecuted Christians worldwide. www.opendoorsuk.org

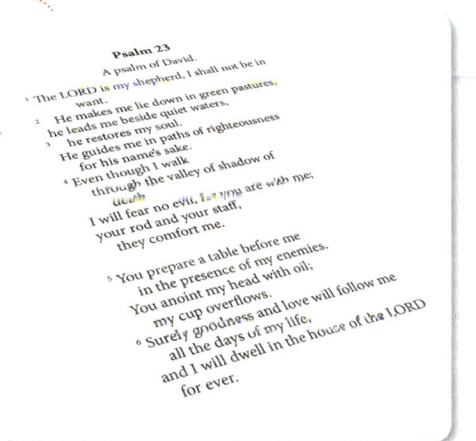

Psalm 23
A psalm of David.
1. The LORD is my shepherd, I shall not be in want.
2. He makes me lie down in green pastures, he leads me beside quiet waters,
3. he restores my soul. He guides me in paths of righteousness for his name's sake.
4. Even though I walk through the valley of shadow of death, I will fear no evil, for you are with me; your rod and your staff, they comfort me.
5. You prepare a table before me in the presence of my enemies. You anoint my head with oil; my cup overflows.
6. Surely goodness and love will follow me all the days of my life, and I will dwell in the house of the LORD for ever.

ACTIVITY 41

(a) After reading Hea Woo's story, share with one person your reactions to it.
(b) Talk about what it was that you think kept her going in these harsh and difficult conditions.
(c) Now read Psalm 23. Bearing in mind that in North Korea you cannot have Bibles or obviously Christian things, devise a visual image that would give the main parts of the psalm, and which could be used for meditating on, without being found out by the guards. Using the template grid provided, plan out what you need to include. Think about the main images in the psalm, and what pictures you could use to represent them. Arrange them in a way so that 'reading' the picture would help a prisoner and any friends in the camp. Then create your image. (There is a template for the image if you wish to use it, but you can devise your own.)
(d) Look back at the material you wrote for Activity 37. Consider whether the things you wrote, about what and who helped you during your hard time, would help you during the sort of hardship Hea Woo, and others like her, face.
(d) Write a prayer, or a wish statement, as a response to Hea Woo's request. Perhaps make a class display of these prayers/wishes.

It might seem quite far-fetched that people can endure such hardships and trials. Yet history and human experience is full of examples which demonstrate that people with a faith, something they believe in that really matters to them and gives them meaning and purpose in their lives, can and do survive extraordinary situations.

So what is it about faith that gives people that drive and determination to overcome difficulties and not give up?

Another example from the Bible might give us a clue. You have probably heard of Daniel in the lion's den, but this is a story that involves three of Daniel's friends (Daniel 3: 1 - 30)

The King of Babylon, Nebuchadnezzar made a great gold statue of one of his gods. It was twenty seven metres high and nearly three metres wide. All the important people – governors, councillors, magistrates – went to the dedication of the statue. The best musicians were there, with pipes and lyres and harps.

'As soon as the music starts, everyone is to bow down and worship the god,' said the king, 'or I'll have him burnt to death in the hottest furnace.'

They all did as they were told; all, that is, except for Daniel's three friends {Shadrach, Meshach and Abednego}. (Daniel himself remained at the royal court.)

The king was furious that they had not bowed down, and asked them what they meant by their defiance. They spoke bravely to the king: 'Our God is able to save us from the fire. Nothing is too hard for Him. But even if he does not save us, we will not worship any other god. We will not bow down to the statue."

The king was now in such a fury that he had the furnace made seven times hotter than usual. The three men were bound hand and foot and thrown into the furnace. It was so hot that the king's men who were throwing them into it were burnt to death themselves.

Suddenly, the king rubbed his eyes in amazement. He could see four men, not three, walking calmly through the flames! 'And the fourth one,' the king said, 'looks like a god!' 'Come out!' he called, and the three friends came out. They were no longer tied up. The flames had not touched their clothes or burnt a hair of their heads! They did not even smell of smoke.

'The God who can do this is indeed a great God,' said the king. 'Let no one say a word against the God of these men.'

ACTIVITY 42

(a) Using a printed copy of the story or a copy on the white board, discuss the following questions as a class:
  1. Which phrase or words indicate the depth of faith of the three men? Explain why.
  2. Why do you think the king found the men's faith so infuriating?
  3. Who do you think was the most surprised by what happened in the furnace?
  4. What phrase or words indicate the result or outcome of the three men's determined faith? Explain why.

(b) Read again the psalm that the North Korean woman meditated on every day. What in the psalm could be illustrated in this story? Write out the phrase, or your explanation of it.

Psalm 23

A psalm of David.

1 The LORD is my shepherd, I shall not be in want.
2 He makes me lie down in green pastures,
he leads me beside quiet waters,
3 he restores my soul.
He guides me in paths of righteousness
for his name's sake.
4 Even though I walk
through the valley of shadow of death,
I will fear no evil, for you are with me;
your rod and your staff,
they comfort me.

5 You prepare a table before me
in the presence of my enemies.
You anoint my head with oil;
my cup overflows.
6 Surely goodness and love will follow me
all the days of my life,
and I will dwell in the house of the LORD
for ever.

When faith is tested to the limit, as in some of the examples we have covered, the outcome of endurance, achievement, success, or whatever it is, is powerful proof that conviction makes a difference. This brings us almost full circle, to the start of this book, where we began thinking about the power of belief.

We end with three more stories that help to illustrate the tremendous power of deeply held faith, or conviction, that endures and outlasts attempts to defeat and destroy it.

THE STORY OF ELIE WIESEL

Elie Wiesel was born to a Jewish family in a region of Romania that was then called Transylvania.

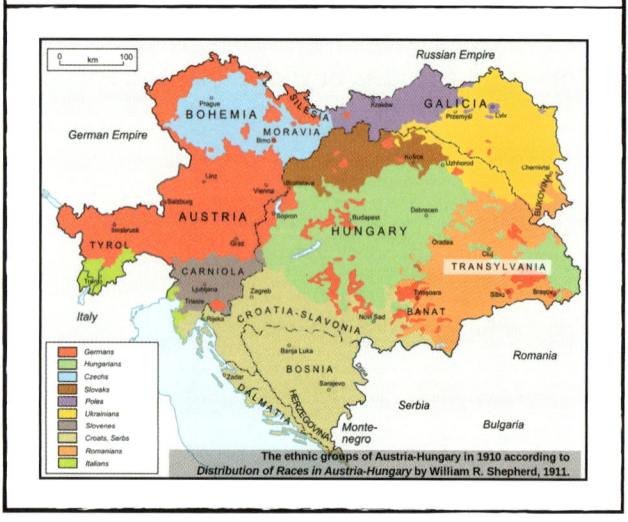

At the age of 15, he and his family were deported by the Nazis to Auschwitz. His father, mother and younger sister all died there.

After the war, Elie became a journalist, and one day, during an interview, was persuaded to write about his experiences in the Nazi death camps. As a result, he published a very successful memoir entitled *Night*, which has been translated into more than 30 different languages. He has written more than 60 books.

After going into teaching and lecturing, at the age of 44 he was appointed Distinguished Professor of Judaic Studies at the City University of New York.

He is a devoted supporter of Israel, but he has also defended other causes to do with human rights and justice all over the world.

In 1986, Elie was awarded the Nobel Prize for Peace, and soon after he and his wife Marian set up the Elie Wiesel Foundation for Humanity. This organisation fights indifference, intolerance and injustice.

Elie has received more than a hundred honorary degrees from institutions of higher learning. He is currently Professor in Humanity at Boston University.

"The opposite of love is not hate, it's indifference. The opposite of art is not ugliness, it's indifference. The opposite of faith is not heresy, it's indifference. The opposite of life is not death, it's indifference."
(Elie Wiesel)

"What unites us as human beings is the aspiration to make the world better, more compassionate, with less conflict, less hate and hardship, and with more tolerance and understanding."
(Elie Wiesel)

THE STORY OF AUNG SAN SUU KYI

Aung San Suu Kyi was born to a Buddhist family in 1945 in Rangoon, capital of Burma, or Myanmar, as it is now known. (Many human rights activists prefer to use the name Burma, as Myanmar was imposed on the country by the current government which the activists do not recognise as legitimate).

She was educated in India and England, and attended university at Oxford. She married a British citizen, Michael Aris, a Tibetan scholar. They had two children, Alexander and Kim. Aung San Suu Kyi's father was the founder of Burma (Myanmar), but was assassinated in 1947. Political oppression followed soon afterwards, and in 1962 a military dictatorship took control.

In 1988, Aung San Suu Kyi returned to Burma to nurse her mother who was dying. At the time, pro-democracy demonstrations were taking place, and were brutally repressed. Because of her strong Buddhist principles, Aung San Suu Kyi spoke out against the military government's activities. She believed strongly in the principles of non-violent protest, and worked tirelessly for human rights, democracy and freedom in Burma.

Her mother died in the December of 1988, and her funeral became a peaceful protest against the non-democratic government. In 1989 Aung San Suu Kyi became the democratically elected leader, winning 80% of the seats in the election, but the military rulers refused to allow the parliament to be formed. They put Aung San Suu Kyi under house arrest.

"If you're feeling helpless, help someone."
(Aung San Suu Kyi)

This did not stop her from fighting for the things she believed in and in 1991 she was awarded the Nobel Prize for Peace. She set up a health and education trust with the prize money. She was released from house arrest in 1995, but not allowed to leave the country, and she was closely monitored by the regime.

In 1999 Michael, her husband whom she had not seen for three years, died of cancer on his 53rd birthday. The regime had not allowed Michael to enter the country to see his wife before he died, and she refused to leave the country for fear that the regime would prevent her from returning afterwards.

She was finally released from her third period of detention on 13th November 2010, and in January the following year she registered as a candidate for a seat in parliament. In April 2012 she won her election, and duly took up her seat in May 2012. She is currently the opposition leader in the parliament. Throughout her years of detention and house arrest, she refused to give up her strong beliefs in non-violent protest and standing up for justice, democracy and freedom.

"My top priority is for people to understand that they have the power to change things themselves."
(Aung San Suu Kyi)

"The only real prison is fear, and the only real freedom is freedom from fear."
(Aung San Suu Kyi)

THE STORY OF SOLOMON NORTHUP

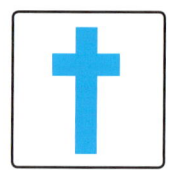

(PORTRAYED IN THE FILM '12 YEARS A SLAVE').

In 1841 Solomon Northup lived in Saratoga Springs, New York, with his wife and two children. He was a free negro, and worked as a skilled carpenter and violinist. One day, two men offered him a two week job as a musician, and promised a good salary and benefits in return. However, they drug Solomon, and when he awakes, he is in a cell, chained and manacled. Despite his statements about who and what he is, he is, after much beating to subdue him, sold as a slave.

He is shipped to New Orleans, and is renamed 'Platt' - a name of a runaway slave from Georgia, who's identity Solomon is forced to accept. Again he is beaten repeatedly, and is finally sold by slave trader Theophilus Freeman to William Ford, the owner of a plantation. Solomon is determined to survive, and gets on well with his master. He even uses his past experience and skills from working on the building of the Champlain Canal (which links Lake Champlain to Hudson River in New York) to construct a waterway for transporting logs swiftly and more cheaply down stream. William Ford is grateful for this helpful contribution, and presents Solomon with a violin, and looks forward to future collaboration.

Unfortunately, one of Ford's overseers, John Tibeats, takes a dislike to Solomon, and continually applies pressure and unnecessary complaints over his work. Eventually, Tibeats attacks Solomon, who fights back. Although saved by a higher overseer, Solomon is eventually strung up in a lynch, and left supporting himself on tip toes, almost strangling. William Ford, on returning to the plantation, cuts the rope and frees him, but tells him he has to go and become a slave to William Epps. Ford could not guarantee Solomon's safety, and so had sold him on.

William Epps owns a cotton plantation, and his slaves are required to pick cotton each day. Each slave is required to pick at least 200 pounds of cotton every day, or they are given a beating with a whip. Epps also believed he had the right to abuse his slaves, which he regarded as has his possessions, and that this right was stated in the Bible. Many of the negro slaves were Christians themselves, and their spiritual songs helped to give them some comfort. Solomon begins to join in the singing and believes with a renewed strength that the time would come when he could be free again.

One day, an outbreak of cotton worm attacks the plants, and Epps is convinced this is a plague sent by God because of the slaves. He leases them out to a neighbouring sugar plantation owner. Solomon again works hard, and eventually gains the favour of the owner, who allows him to play the violin at a wedding anniversary celebration, and keep the money he earns. Soon after, the slaves are returned to Epps, and Solomon attempts to use the money to pay a white field hand and former overseer to post a letter to Solomon's friends in Saratoga Springs. The man agrees, accepts the money and tells Solomon to write his letter. However, he betrays Solomon, who only just manages to persuade Epps that it was a lie; but he has to burn the letter, and so loose another opportunity to bring about his freedom.

Another opportunity comes when a Canadian carpenter, named Bass, is employed by Epps to build a gazebo near the plantation house. Solomon is assigned to help Bass, and on hearing him state his views against slavery to Epps, is encouraged to confide in him. Solomon asks Bass to deliver a letter for him to Saratoga Springs, which was a risky thing to undertake. Bass agrees, because he sees the way Epps treats his slaves.

One day, many weeks later, a local sheriff arrives with a man and calls Solomon over. After a few questions, he is able to match up Solomon - called Platt since he was first sold - with the facts he has been given. Solomon recognises the man with the sheriff as the shopkeeper whom he knew well, back in Saratoga Springs. William Epps of course resists the freeing of one of his slaves, but Solomon is taken away by the sheriff and has new papers stating his free status.

Solomon returns to his family, and tries to rebuild something of his life. He had spent 12 years as a slave, but despite lengthy legal battles in the courts, he was never able to prosecute, or get convicted, the men who were responsible for selling him into slavery.

"Life is dear to every living thing; the worm that crawls upon the ground will struggle for it." (Solomon Northup)

"Place ... (a person) in the midst of dangers, cut him off from human aid, let the grave open before him, then it is, in the time of his tribulation, that the scoffer and unbelieving man turns to God for help, feeling there is no other hope, or refuge, or safety, save in His protecting arm."
(Solomon Northup)

ACTIVITY 43

Using one of the stories, your team of 10 will be working in pairs. Your task is to jointly produce a stunning explanatory poster. Each pair will have a specific responsibility for one fifth of the poster. The task for each pair is to read the appropriate story, and think about the words and images that would be appropriate to visually demonstrate the aspect they have been given, using the templates provided. Each template will fit together to comprise the total picture/collage. When completed, the team can present the story and its explanation to the rest of the class, using their poster.

Finally, complete an evaluation of these three examples of faith and determination, using these headings:
- the most challenging example
- three things in common between all three examples
- something unique in each example
- why you think each managed to achieve what they did
- the quotation you found the most stimulating/surprising, and why.

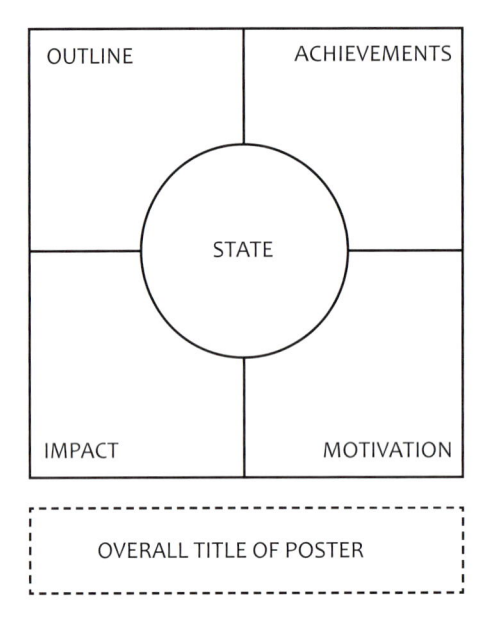

```
┌─────────────┬─────────────┐
│  OUTLINE    │ ACHIEVEMENTS│
│             │             │
│       ╱─────────╲         │
│      │   STATE   │        │
│       ╲─────────╱         │
│             │             │
│  IMPACT     │  MOTIVATION │
└─────────────┴─────────────┘
      ┌ ─ ─ ─ ─ ─ ─ ─ ─ ┐
        OVERALL TITLE OF POSTER
      └ ─ ─ ─ ─ ─ ─ ─ ─ ┘
```

The focus for each pair is to devise and create words and images that cover the aspects in the table below.

S	**STATE** – who the person is, where they live/lived, their religious stance/background	Pair 1
O	**OUTLINE** – what they experienced – in brief	Pair 2
A	**ACHIEVEMENTS** – what were their main achievements	Pair 3
I	**IMPACT** – of their faith on what they did and how they responded	Pair 4
M	**MOTIVATION** – what kept them going, gave them the determination to fight on, survive, succeed?	Pair 5

Summing up: Does faith stand the test?

We accepted that culture has an important influence on a person's faith and beliefs, and considered how these are things that really matter to most people. Inevitably though, the principles, beliefs, or faith by which you live your life will be tested – by others, by experiences and hardships in life, by rules, governments, and authorities.

The Bible gives an image that is useful here:

'I have tested you in the fire of suffering,
as silver is refined in a furnace …' (Isaiah 48: 10)

'(The) purpose (of sufferings and trials) is to prove that your faith is genuine.
Even gold, which can be destroyed, is tested by fire;
and so your faith, which is much more precious than gold,
must also be tested so that it may endure.' (1 Peter 1: 7)

And when a person's faith or belief is something deep and meaningful, then it enables him/her to face opposition and oppression with a powerful conviction that is evidence of its own proof.

UNIT 4
FAITH IN A MULTICULTURAL SOCIETY

Engage with fundamental questions:

What is a multicultural society?

Why are there a variety of beliefs in Wales?

How do we value difference?

Why do we need to protect diversity?

Explore Beliefs,

- The variety of belief systems in Wales.
- You should treat others as you want to be treated.

Teachings

- To continue the religion through passing on the message to either your own children or other people.
- Various religious teachings on equality.

and Practices

- The growth of religions in Wales and the world.

Express:

Using your own opinions along with what you have found out …

What is a multicultural society?

Why are there a variety of beliefs in Wales?

How do we value difference?

Why do we need to protect diversity?

Religions in Wales in the 21st Century

The population of the UK is around 65 million people. The population of Wales is just over 3 million. A census is an official survey or questionnaire usually completed by the population of a whole nation. According to the Office of National Statistics (ONS), there has been a census in England and Wales every ten years since 1801, except for 1941, because of the Second World War. Although there was a question about religion in the 1851 census (UK population: 20 Million), reports focused entirely on different denominations within Christianity, with the addition of Judaism. It wasn't until 2001 that a question asking about a person's religion was included in the main section of the census. In reports available from the ONS website the numbers for the 6 main world religions are given.

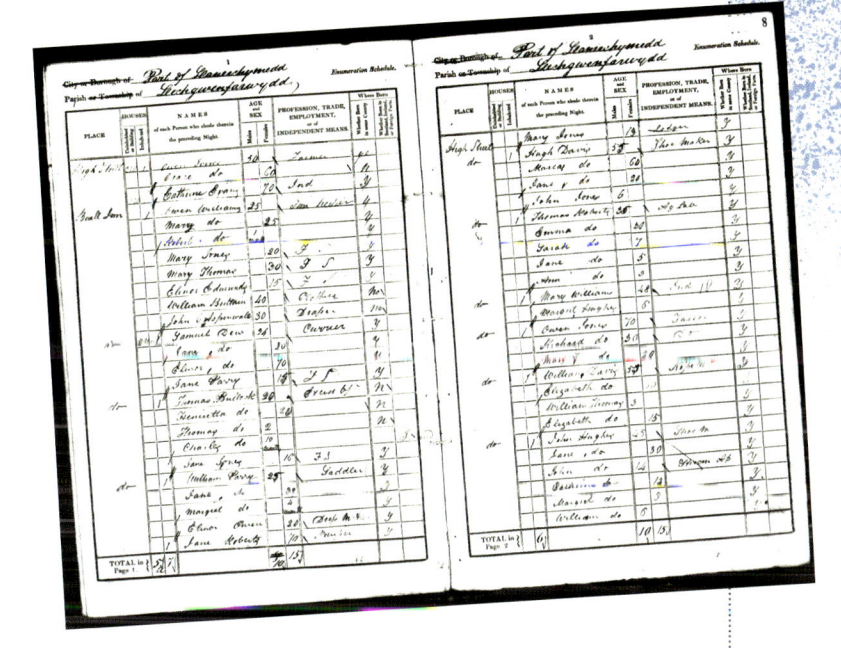

ACTIVITY 44

a) List the 6 religions which you think are mentioned on the ONS website.
b) In a group, then as a class, compare your lists. (Answer on page 91)
c) Place the 7 belief systems, including 'non-religious', in order of the number of followers they have in Wales, as you think they would have been in the 2011 census. (Answer on page 91)

There are many more religions and belief systems than these 6 religions. The ONS include two other categories when reporting on religions in England and Wales. These are 'religious other', relating to those who follow religions other than the main six, and 'non-religious', including atheists, agnostics and others who may not follow a traditional belief system.

ACTIVITY 45

a) Write down two reasons why you think that the Office for National Statistics only reports on these 6 religions.
b) In a group, then as a class, create a list of these reasons and discuss which are most likely.

World religion

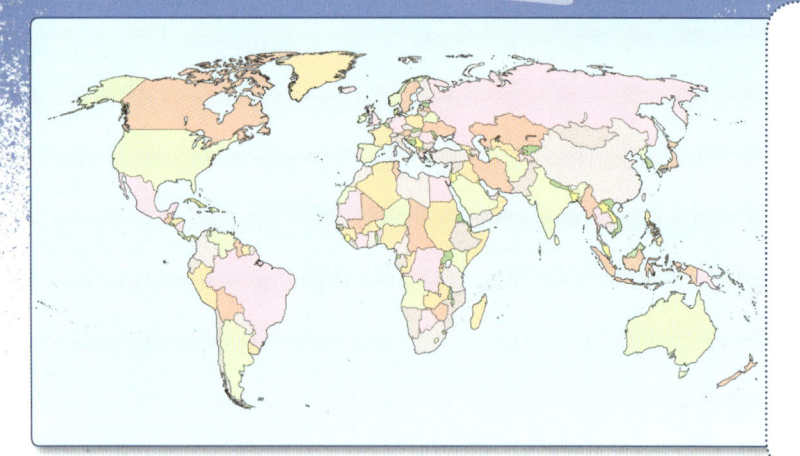

Before we look at the religions in Wales, we will consider how important they are around the world. Christianity, Islam, Hinduism, Sikhism, Judaism and Buddhism are considered as the world's '6 main world religions'. The following activity will help you to find out how many followers each religion has across the world. All numbers in this activity are based on approximations.

ACTIVITY 46

a) In pairs, use a set of similar cards and arrange them in a way that shows the number of followers for each belief system.
b) One card is incomplete. Work out which religion it is, the number of followers and the percentage (%) of the world's population.
c) Discuss as a class the ways in which you could work out the percentages (%) and numbers of followers for the incomplete card.
d) Discuss as a class:
   i. Are there any figures you expected?
   ii. Are there any figures that surprised you?

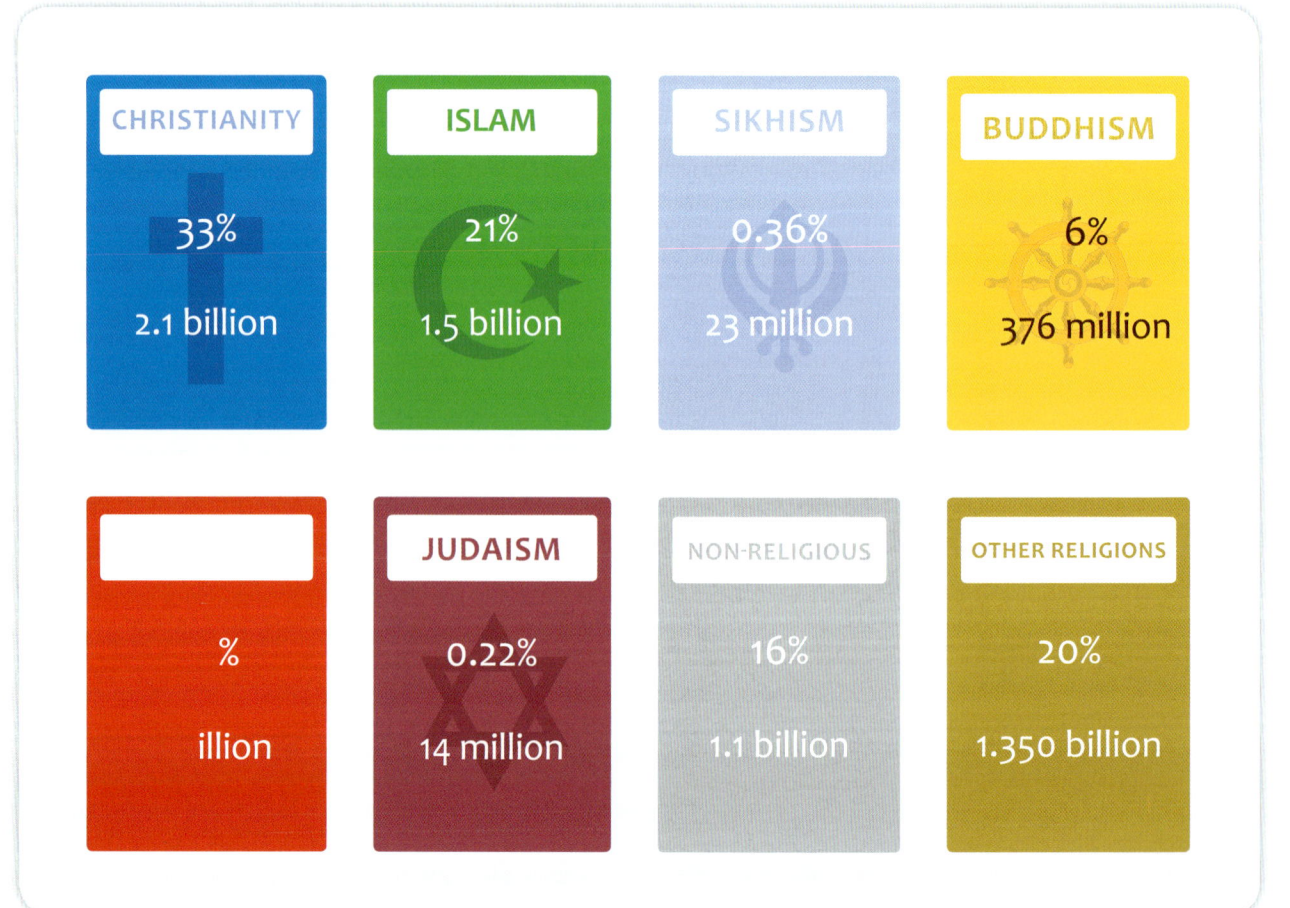

CHRISTIANITY	ISLAM	SIKHISM	BUDDHISM
33%	21%	0.36%	6%
2.1 billion	1.5 billion	23 million	376 million

	JUDAISM	NON-RELIGIOUS	OTHER RELIGIONS
%	0.22%	16%	20%
illion	14 million	1.1 billion	1.350 billion

ACTIVITY 47

In the challenge section are groups of people within different religions.
  a) Arrange the challenge cards with the main world religion cards in a way that shows the groups within the different religions.
  b) One challenge card is incomplete. Work out which group it is, the number of followers and the percentage (%) of the world's population.

The following information may help you ...

Estimated world population: 6.638 billion (6,638,000,000 or six billion, six hundred and thirty eight million)

thousand – 1,000
million – 1,000,000
billion – 1,000,000,000

Groups within a religion

CHRISTIANITY

PROTESTANT
34%
700 million

EASTERN ORTHODOX
11%
230 million

%
llllon

ISLAM

SUNNI
90%
1.350 billion

SHIA
10%
150 million

BUDDHISM

THERAVADA
29%
110 million

MAHAYANA
56%
210 million

TIBETAN
6%
20 million

OTHER BUDDHIST GROUPS
9%
36 million

71

Why have the religions grown in number?

In unit 2 we looked at the beginnings of these 6 main world religions. Most of them began as the result of one person. Even though Christianity was started by Jesus over 2000 years ago, 1/3 of the people in the world consider his teachings to be important. How did relatively few people affect the lives of the whole world?

ACTIVITY 48

Which of the following actions would you consider asking others to do and which would you think should be kept within a family?

- using less water
- parents giving their children money for doing well in an examination
- washing hands before having a meal
- walking instead of using the car whenever possible
- praying together before having a meal
- being welcomed into a religion (e.g. Christening)
- creating a quick exit plan for a home in case there is a fire
- a grandfather passing on his old watch to someone else

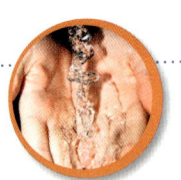

> When I was growing up my family always had bread rolls with pork and stuffing on Christmas Eve. I thought it was a tradition that everybody did, like Christmas trees and putting up decorations. I didn't find out that it was just a family tradition until I got married and my wife hadn't considered putting pork on our Christmas shopping list. We now have our own family version of this tradition.

ACTIVITY 49

Can you explain any tradition your family has? For example, do you do something as a family that other families don't?

Whilst there are many reasons why religions have grown, we are going to focus on two:

Passing it on to others
Religious followers may want to spread the 'message' of the religion on to others. Some may consider the message so important that they must pass it on – not passing it on is putting others in danger of punishment from God. Others may think that their message would improve the lives of other people, and that it is, therefore, a loving thing to tell them.

Keeping it in the family
Followers may pass on their religious traditions to their children to ensure that the beliefs and actions continue with the next generation.

Most religious people who share their religious message will pass it on to their family.

ACTIVITY 50

Read each of the following quotations and decide whether it supports:
- a) spreading the message of the founder to others;
- b) passing on the teachings within their own community.

▶ Christianity
Jesus said, "Go and make disciples of all nations, baptising them in the name of the Father and of the Son and of the Holy Spirit, and teaching them to obey everything I have commanded you." (Matthew 28:19-20)

▶ Islamic statement of faith
'There is no God but Allah and Muhammad is his messenger.'

▶ Buddhism
'You can achieve the end of suffering if you follow the teachings of the Buddha.'

▶ Judaism
'You are a Jew if your mother is a Jew.'

▶ Hinduism
'The term Hindu comes from the name given to the people living in Indus Valley. Hinduism is more a way of life rather than a belief.'

▶ Sikhism
'The kirpan or sword worn by Sikhs symbolises the protection of the Sikh community's beliefs and the protection of the weak no matter what they believe.'

Religions in Wales

Because religions have grown in number and spread around the world, it is no surprise that there is a variety of religions in Wales. We will now explore the number of people in Wales who consider themselves part of these religions.

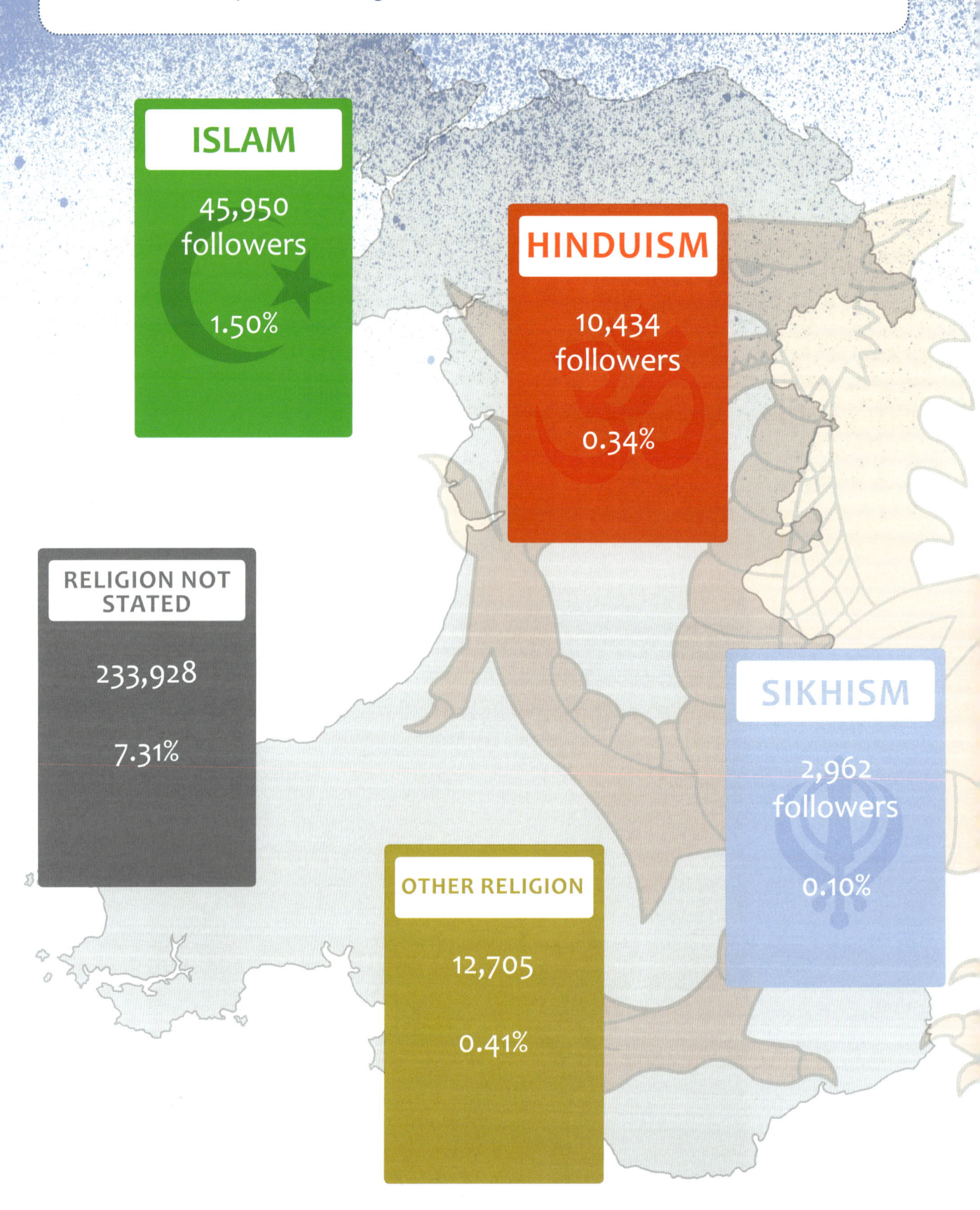

ISLAM
45,950 followers
1.50%

HINDUISM
10,434 followers
0.34%

RELIGION NOT STATED
233,928
7.31%

SIKHISM
2,962 followers
0.10%

OTHER RELIGION
12,705
0.41%

ACTIVITY 51

a) One card is incomplete. Work out which religion it is, the number of followers and the percentage (%) of the Welsh population.

b) Discuss as a class the ways in which you could work out the percentage (%) and number of followers for the incomplete card.

c) Discuss as a class:
   a. Are there any figures you expected?
   b. Are there any figures that surprised you?

d) Discuss the various graphs or charts you could use to present this data. Which one would you choose and why?

The following information may help you …

Population of Wales according to the 2011 census: 3,063,456 (or three million, sixty three thousand, four hundred and fifty six)

thousand	– 1,000
ten thousand	– 10,000
hundred thousand	– 100,000
million	– 1,000,000

BUDDHISM

9,117 followers

0.30%

NOT RELIGIOUS

982,997

32.10%

JUDAISM

2,064 followers

0.07%

Why are there different religious beliefs in Wales?

So we have considered how many people in Wales have religious beliefs. But why are there different religious beliefs in Wales? To answer this we will have to look at the history of both Wales and the UK.

timeline

Christianity

Before I became a Roman soldier, I used to live in Rome. I became a Christian after hearing the message about Jesus' resurrection from the dead. In 60AD I signed up to be a soldier and was sent with my legion to Briton (where Wales, northern England and southern Scotland is today, and where the Celtic people then lived). We attacked and defeated the druids in Anglesey. By 80AD we had conquered the whole of England and Wales.

Islam

Hi, my name is Aamir and I'm 15 years old. I was born in an Arab country called Yemen but we moved to Cardiff in 1871. My dad is a docker, which means he loads ships for a living. The opening of the Suez Canal in 1861 meant that boats could travel carrying goods from Arab countries through to the Mediterranean Sea and out into the Atlantic. It meant that Arab countries could trade with Europe, including the UK. My dad heard of work in Cardiff and we moved. A few of us Muslims from Yemen and other Arab countries would meet to say our prayers on Fridays.

Sikhism

I was a foundry worker in the Punjab, India. One day when I was at work, I heard that some of my colleagues had gone to the UK to work in the foundries in some of the big cities. The British government had been encouraging people from the colonies, like me, to come to the UK and help rebuild the country after the Second World War. So in the summer of 1952 I left the Punjab to start a new life in the UK.

Judaism

According to my grandad, Jews had lived in the UK since Roman times. He said that there are records of Jewish settlements dating from William the Conqueror. My grandad left Austria in the 1930's; he said that people were becoming wary of Jews in Austria. He decided to make a new, 'safer' life for himself in the UK. He met Grandma at the local synagogue; her family had come to the UK years before.

Buddhism

My name is Cheng Lee. My father was originally from Hong Kong, but he worked all over the world as a captain on big ships. In 1869 we moved to the UK and settled in Cardiff. My dad spent more time docked in the port here than in China, which meant we were able to spend more time with him. We have always followed the teachings of the Buddha. (In the 1861 census, 147 Chinese born residents were living in England and Wales.)

Hinduism

My dad is a doctor. He said that we had to go to the UK as the NHS was having problems getting enough doctors. We moved in 1962 and my dad started working in the local hospital. We found many Hindus who had come over in the 1940's to help the UK after the war. Many Hindus left India to find better paid work in the UK.

Hindus visited the UK in the 19th century. In 1888, Mahatma Gandhi, a famous Hindu, began studying law in England.

ACTIVITY 52

a) Create a time-line of religions in Wales.
b) Explain why we have a variety of religions in Wales and the reasons they came to Wales.
c) Extension: Methodism is a denomination within Christianity. When, how and why did it start?

Value in difference

We have explored the variety of religions in Wales and it is clear that there are large numbers of people with different beliefs. These beliefs affect the way they dress, act and behave. Before we look at the value in having these differences, it is important to discuss the teachings these religions have on equality. Equality for people of different beliefs can be found in valuing the importance of a person rather than the importance of the beliefs he/she holds. Whilst many religions disagree with the beliefs held by other religions, the vast majority respect a person's right to hold those beliefs.

The Parable of the Good Samaritan

Luke 10:25-37

25 On one occasion an expert in the law stood up to test Jesus. "Teacher," he asked, "what must I do to inherit eternal life?"

26 "What is written in the Law?" he replied. "How do you read it?"

27 He answered, "'Love the Lord your God with all your heart and with all your soul and with all your strength and with all your mind'; and, 'Love your neighbour as yourself.'"

28 "You have answered correctly," Jesus replied. "Do this and you will live."

29 But he wanted to justify himself, so he asked Jesus, "And who is my neighbour?"

30 In reply Jesus said: "A man was going down from Jerusalem to Jericho, when he was attacked by robbers. They stripped him of his clothes, beat him and went away, leaving him half dead. 31 A priest happened to be going down the same road, and when he saw the man, he passed by on the other side. 32 So too, a Levite, when he came to the place and saw him, passed by on the other side. 33 But a Samaritan, as he travelled, came where the man was; and when he saw him, he took pity on him. 34 He went to him and bandaged his wounds, pouring on oil and wine. Then he put the man on his own donkey, brought him to an inn and took care of him.

35 The next day he took out two denarii* and gave them to the innkeeper. 'Look after him,' he said, 'and when I return, I will reimburse you for any extra expense you may have.'

36 "Which of these three do you think was a neighbour to the man who fell into the hands of robbers?"

37 The expert in the law replied, "The one who had mercy on him."

Jesus told him, "Go and do likewise."

* Roman currency about 211 BC

(NIV)

Extra information:

When Jesus told this parable, the first people to hear it would have been Jews who despised the Samaritans. The Samaritans were a group of people who lived near but had different beliefs and customs. The priest and Levite who walked on the other side were religious Jews who should have helped the man who had been mugged. They would have been very surprised to hear Jesus say that they should be nice to those who hate them.

ACTIVITY 53

What was Jesus really saying with this story? Include references from the story in your answer.

All of the main world religions have teachings that support the need to treat each other with respect.

In a survey of attitudes towards religions amongst young people in the UK, young people who belonged to a major world religion were more tolerant of other religions in the UK than those young people who said they had no religion.

ACTIVITY 54

a) Does the above statement surprise you?
b) Would you expect people who have a religious belief to be more or less tolerant than those without religious belief? Give reasons for your answer.

The following are teachings from the main world religions on the topic of equality.

Christianity

Bible: Mark 12:31

Love your neighbour as yourself.

Bible: Luke 6:31

Do to others as you would have them do unto you.

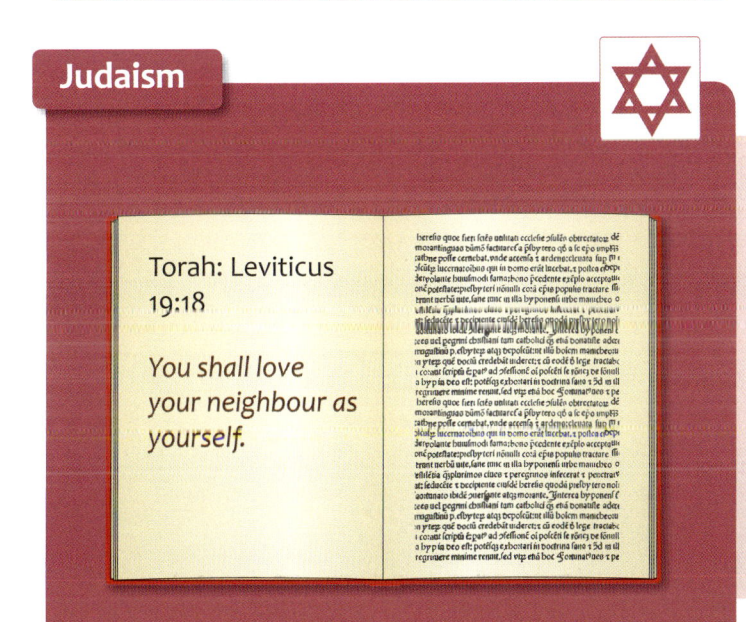

Judaism

Torah: Leviticus 19:18

You shall love your neighbour as yourself.

Tanach: Malachi 2:10

Have we not all one father? Has not one God created us?

Islam

Qur'an: Surah 49:19

O mankind! We created you out of a single pair of male and female, and We made you into different nations and tribes so that you may get to know and love one another. Not that you may despise each other.

Quotation from the prophet Muhammad:

'Your God is one and your forefather (Adam) is one. An Arab is not better than a non-Arab and a non-Arab is not better than an Arab, and a white person is not better than a black person and a black person is not better than a white person, except in piety'.

Sikhism

Guru Granth Sahib Ji: 349-13

Recognise the Lord's light within all, and do not consider social class or status; there are no classes in the world hereafter.

Guru Granth Sahib Ji: 435

All beings and creatures are His; He belongs to all.

Hinduism

Bhagavad Gita 9.29

I look upon all creatures equally; none are less important to me and none more important.

Bhagavad Gita 9.32-33

All those who take refuge in me, whatever their birth, race, sex, or caste, will attain the supreme goal; this realisation can be attained even by those whom society hates. Kings and sages too seek this goal with devotion.

Buddhism

Tripitaka: Sutta Nipata 648

So what of all these titles, names, and races? They are only made up by man.

Quotation from Hui Neng (important Buddhist Monk, born 638AD)

'Although there are northern men and southern men, north and south make no difference to their Buddha-nature. A barbarian is different from you physically, but there is no difference in our Buddha-nature.'

ACTIVITY 55

a) Read through the teachings from the world religions regarding equality.
b) Choose 2 religions and explain why the majority of their followers believe it is important to be tolerant of other people's religious beliefs.

In Unit 2 we engaged with the question of culture. Culture involves many of the similarities that a group of people share. But even within the same culture there will be differences.

ACTIVITY 56

a) Answer all of the following questions:
   a. What is your favourite colour?
   b. What is your favourite food?
   c. What subject are you good at?
   d. What music don't you like?
   e. Where are your grandparents from?
b) Ask 4 other pupils to answer the same questions.
c) Compare your answers.

Wales is a multicultural society, which means that there are many people from different cultures living together. If each culture has its differences, then a multicultural society will have people with very different beliefs living alongside each other. To be able to value each other in a multicultural society it is important to respect each other's beliefs.

ACTIVITY 57

Complete a similar table of the various differences that we have explored throughout this book.

Hindus worship in a mandir

570CE Makkah

Siddhartha Gautama

Jesus

Muslims worship in a mosque

Guru Nanak

Muhammad

Abraham

2500BCE Indus Valley

500BCE North East India

30CE Israel

Qur'an

1469CE Punjab

	symbol	holy buildings
Buddhism		
Christianity		
Hinduism		
Islam		
Judaism		
Sikhism		

Buddhists worship in a temple

Tripitaka

Bible

holy book	founder	started date/where

Vedas

Jews worship in a synagogue

Torah

No founder

Guru Granth Sahib

2000BCE Israel

Sikhs worship in a gurdwara

Christians worship in a church or chapel

Valuing difference is to recognise and celebrate cultural differences whilst understanding and respecting the fact that we are all human. As Wales is a multicultural country, it is important to reflect on the benefits that multiculturalism brings.

The benefits of multiculturalism:

- The opportunity to see very different cultures without having to travel too far around the world 
- Different cultures view the world in a different way; learning about other people's beliefs helps me to work out what I think. 
- Artistic taste from different cultures may be very different. Music, fashion and films from other cultures have all inspired what happens in the UK. 
- Foods from other cultures are now available to all. 
- As people share their lives together, there is an understanding of other cultures rather than just a knowledge. 
- An increased richness to the English vocabulary (e.g. 'pyjama' is a Hindu word.)

ACTIVITY 58

Design an ICT presentation showing the benefits of multiculturalism. You must include references to some of the 6 benefits highlighted above.

Protecting our diversity

ACTIVITY 59

Look at the two quotations below. Discuss with a partner the positive effects and the negative effects that these statements could cause.

> I should be able to say what I want.

> I should be able to do what I want.

The European Convention on Human Rights (ECHR) is an agreed list, or treaty, of basic human rights that were created in the 1950's to help protect people's freedom. Articles in the treaty cover issues such as the right to life and to liberty. Article 9 states:

1. Everyone has the right to freedom of thought, conscience and religion; this right includes freedom to change his religion or belief, and freedom, either alone or in community with others and in public or private, to manifest his religion or belief, in worship, teaching, practice and observance.

2. Freedom to manifest one's religion or beliefs shall be subject only to such limitations as are prescribed by law and are necessary in a democratic society in the interests of public safety, for the protection of public order, health or morals, or for the protection of the rights and freedoms of others.

ACTIVITY 60

a) Do you think that it is important that everyone should be able to act on their beliefs? Give reasons for your answer.
b) Does Article 9 enable people to act on their beliefs whilst protecting people with other beliefs? Which bit of the article supports this?

We stated earlier that equality for people of different beliefs can be found in valuing the importance of a person rather than the importance of the beliefs he/she holds. Whilst many religions disagree with the beliefs held by other religions, the vast majority respect a person's right to hold those beliefs. This is supported by the ECHR. Article 9 defends the right to act on a person's beliefs whilst at the same time protecting the rights of other people.

In a multicultural society many people with different beliefs are living alongside one another, so is there a need to protect this diversity in the UK? In 1976 the Race Relations Act was made law in order to protect people from being discriminated against on the basis of race, nationality, religious beliefs and ethnicity. More recently, the Racial and Religious Hatred Act 2006 made it a crime to promote hatred towards someone based on religious or racial grounds.

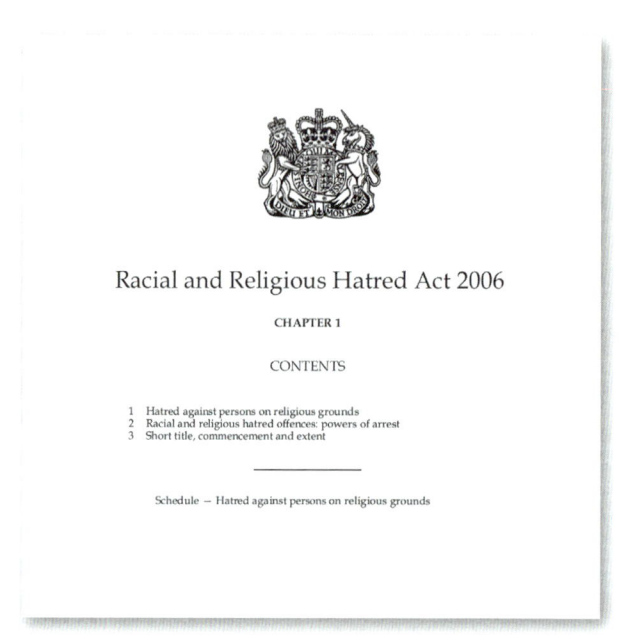

The Diary of Anne Frank

Anne Frank pictured in May 1942

Statue of Anne Frank, by Mari Andriessen, outside the Westerkerk in Amsterdam

Reconstruction of the bookcase that covered the entrance to the secret annex, in the Anne Frank House in Amsterdam

Whilst the Holocaust is an extreme case of the effect of not valuing difference, it highlights the importance of religious and cultural tolerance, especially in a country where there are so many different cultures living alongside one another.

Anne Frank lived at a time when the differences of the Jewish religion weren't valued. The Jews were blamed for a nation that was struggling after the First World War. Adolf Hitler was able to use the differences between the 'culture of Germany' and the Jewish religion to create hatred towards the Jews. Rather than respecting the humanity of all people, the Nazis focused on division. Over 6 million Jews were killed at the hand of the Nazis, many in concentration camps. Anne wrote a diary at the time of these events.

Anne Frank was born in Germany in 1929. Her family moved to Amsterdam, Holland when Anne was a young girl. She was 10 years old when the Nazis invaded the Netherlands in May 1940. Early in the diary she recounts how the Jews were marked out as different, and were made to wear a yellow star. Jews weren't allowed out after 8 o'clock in the evening. She states that they weren't even allowed to visit Christians in their homes. Anne and her sister were moved from a school with non-Jewish children to one where there were only Jews.

Anne's father, a business man, wanted to protect his family and so decided to go into hiding in an annex hidden in the building where he worked. In 1942, two families moved into this annex. They had to be quiet all day and they would not dare to leave as they may be caught by the Nazis. Many of the Jews in Nazi occupied countries were forced to live in ghettos, areas of the city just for Jews. The Jews in these ghettos were then moved to concentration camps.

The diary was a 13th birthday present in 1942, 12 days before entering the annex. It details the events and her thoughts as she spent 2 years in hiding. The diary ends abruptly on 1st August 1944. The family was discovered 3 days later. The two families were sent to concentration camps where all of them except Otto, Anne's father, died. Otto returned to Holland after the war and found the diary. The dairy was published as a book in 1947. A final section was added explaining that Anne and her sister were transported from Auschwitz in Poland at the end of October 1944 and brought to a concentration camp in Germany called Bergen Belsen. She died in the February or March of 1945.

ACTIVITY 61

Many German people were turning against Jews who they had lived and worked alongside for years. Write a diary extract describing how Anne, as a young Jewish girl, would have felt about these Germans. You could include how she felt about not being able to visit her friends because they belonged to a Christian family.

It is difficult to imagine what Anne Frank went through, being persecuted simply because society didn't like her beliefs. But in reading her diary, you get the impression that she understood the balance between staying true to her beliefs and accepting other people's beliefs.

> It's really a wonder that I haven't dropped all my ideals, because they seem so absurd and impossible to carry out. Yet I keep them, because in spite of everything, I still believe that people are really good at heart.

> We all live with the objective of being happy; our lives are all different and yet the same.

> I don't want to have lived in vain like most people. I want to be useful or bring enjoyment to all people, even those I've never met. I want to go on living even after my death!

> People can tell you to keep your mouth shut, but that doesn't stop you from having your own opinion.

(Reproduced by permission of Penguin Books Ltd.)

ACTIVITY 62

Choose one of Anne's quotations and explain how it makes you feel.

Integrity matters

ACTIVITY 63

Write your own definition for the word 'integrity'.

The existence of God for many religious people is more than just a belief; they would go as far as to say that for them it is a fact. They believe in God so much that it affects everything – their beliefs about birth, marriage, death, how they spend their time, money and skills. It is integral to who they are.

As discussed throughout this book, many people don't choose their beliefs – their beliefs are an integral part of who they are. It's difficult to see the world from another point of view. Anne Frank wrote, 'People can tell you to keep your mouth shut, but that doesn't stop you from having your own opinion.' It is important to recognise that other people's beliefs are just as important to them as your beliefs are to you. Anne Frank summed this up: 'We all live with the objective of being happy; our lives are all different and yet the same.'

Many religions have what has been termed 'the Golden Rule':

> Do to others as you would have them do to you.

Freedom to believe and say what you want is important. Protection against discrimination and persecution is equally important.

ACTIVITY 64

Do you think that the Golden Rule would help society to ensure that everybody's rights are protected?

Summing up: Faith in a multicultural society

In this unit we started with the question 'What is a multicultural society?' By looking at the 2011 census data, we have established that Wales is a country made up of a variety of beliefs. We have explored the reasons why there are a variety of faiths. We have also explored the various religious teachings that support the belief that we are all equal before God and each other. By focusing on the value of difference, we also looked at why we may need to protect one another's diversity. We conclude by stating that people's beliefs, however diverse, are so important to the people who hold them. Your beliefs are important to you!

'Although I'm only fourteen, I know quite well what I want, I know who is right and who is wrong. I have my opinions, my own ideas and principles, and although it may sound pretty mad from an adolescent, I feel more of a person than a child, I feel quite independent of anyone.' (Anne Frank)

Final summing up

Hopefully you will have found that the world of beliefs and believing is fascinating. It is not as simple and straightforward as many people assume. Our whole lives are filled with beliefs and expectations, and we make sense of life through them.

Beliefs are therefore powerful influences on what we do, how we think and how we act, and all the choices we make. The beliefs we have are obviously affected by where we live – land and culture. The people we have as parents and relatives, and the heritage that is ours through these people, as well as through our country and religion, also influence our beliefs.

The experiences of life help to strengthen and develop our beliefs; but they can also bring challenges and testing times to our faith. People react differently to these pressures, and some people have a depth and intensity of faith that enables them to maintain their faith in the face of opposition, persecution and hardship.

There is no doubt that we all live in a society of mixed cultures, religion and belief. Responding to this can be positive and beneficial, or divisive and negative. Being in a multicultural environment brings pressures and challenges, as we individually and in different faith or non-faith communities, engage with those who have a different perspective. Such variety can be stimulating and enriching. But, learning to understand that personal faith and conviction is what every person has, means that the integrity of others and their faith systems are acknowledged, so allowing each and all to practise, develop, share, and be proud of their beliefs. It is **believing** that leads to **being** – a human experience that is exciting and rewarding.

Supporting information

ACTIVITY 44 (a)
Christianity
No religion
Islam
Hinduism
Sikhism
Judaism
Buddhism

ACTIVITY 44 (c)
Most   Christianity
           Non-religious
           Islam
           Hinduism
           Buddhism
           Sikhism
Least   Judaism

ACTIVITY 46

Hinduism
175 million
3.42%

ACTIVITY 47

Roman Catholic
1.170 million
55%

ACTIVITY 57

	symbol	holy buildings	holy book	founder	started date/where
Buddhism		temple	Tripitaka	Siddhartha Gautama/ Buddha	500BCE North East India
Christianity		church	Bible	Jesus	30CE Israel
Hinduism		mandir	Vedas	No founder	2500BCE Indus Valley
Islam		mosque	Qur'an	Muhammad	570CE Makkah
Judaism		synagogue	Torah	Abraham	4000 BCE Israel
Sikhism		gurdwara	Guru Granth Sahib	Guru Nanak Dev	1469CE Punjab